Kaylene Brown
design collaboration with Amanda Bagwell
Cover artist Maddie Torres
ISBN: 9798354194728

To Justin, united in soul and body through Christ in the Sacrament of Holy Matrimony. I learned about the love of God through you. I learned I was worthy through your willingness to sacrifice for me and encourage me in my dignity as woman. Ti amo per sempre.
To my children, born and unborn. You are worth more than this world offers. God is making me a saint through the gift of mothering you. Seek first the Kingdom of God.
To Darby, my sister, for her writing and prayers on the week of prayerfulness, and for her overall support and critique. Ruth 1: 16-17.

- Kaylene

∞∞∞∞

Workbook design collaborator Amanda Bagwell lives in Franklin, TN with her husband Jansen, and their four children: Eli, Lindsey, Rachel, and Luke. After both growing up in Protestant ministry, Amanda and Jansen converted to the Catholic faith on Christmas Day, 2014. Together, Jansen and Amanda founded Whole Catholic, where Amanda works as an admin, writer, content creator, and basic doer-of-all-the-things.
Whole Catholic helps individuals move forward in faith and life through a practical, discipleship approach to healing and deliverance.
Find them online at www.WholeCatholic.com

∞∞∞∞

Cover artist Maddie Torres lives in North Carolina with her husband Daniel. He is a Campus minister at a Catholic high school, and she is the brains, artist, and distributor for MrsTorresCreates. Maddie specializes in watercolor saint prints, but also offers stickers and custom prints. Her shop is always expanding and growing. Her art is a visual representation of what has been revealed to her in prayer while creating!
Find her at www.mrstorrescreates.com, and on instagram @mrstorrescreates

∞∞∞∞

Contents

Introduction

Women are the threads that unite society. We foster life and nurture it in others, but when our faith is weak and actions selfish, the Church and the world suffer. We have the power to reflect God's love onto others. Our feminine genius is described as receptive, sensitive, generous, and maternal. Pope St. John Paul II wrote at length on this topic in Mulieris Dignitatem (MD):

> A woman is strong because of her awareness of this entrusting, strong because of the fact that God "entrusts the human being to her", always and in every way, even in the situations of social discrimination in which she may find herself. This awareness and this fundamental vocation speak to women of the dignity which they receive from God himself, and this makes them "strong" and strengthens their vocation. Thus the "perfect woman" becomes an irreplaceable support and source of spiritual strength for other people, who perceive the great energies of her spirit... In this sense, our time in particular awaits the manifestation of that "genius" which belongs to women, and which can ensure sensitivity for human beings in every circumstance: because they are human! - and because "the greatest of these is love." – Pope St. John Paul II

We must first love God, because from Him we receive the strength necessary to care for the whole of humanity. The greatest example of love is Christ on the cross—His loving sacrifice opened the flood of mercy for our redemption. We are all called to follow this example—to will the good of others so much that it makes us uncomfortable by the world's standards; perhaps we even suffer. The word "passion" actually means suffering; so, we acknowledge that true love is hard, but know we aren't left alone! We are able to experience agape love in the Blessed Sacrament. Not only must we love God, but we must allow ourselves to be loved by God.

His True Presence in the Eucharist is the source and summit of a life of grace. Through our receptivity, we consume the Lord and gain strength. We are sensitive to His voice in our souls; hearing His call in prayer. Can we see Him in all that we encounter? Through our feminine genius of generosity, we share our material resources and spiritual experiences. How do we find God in the silence, in the brokenness, in the emptiness of others and our relationships with them? Can we find joy in the love we share, despite our sufferings? The fourth feminine genius component, maternity, is one that aligns most perfectly with Mary's Magnificat and our goal of magnifying the Lord. Her soul magnified the Lord as she was free to literally give birth to Christ. As women striving to more fully live our feminine genius, how do we—in a sense—give birth to Christ for others? Do we magnify Him through our spiritual gift of maternity?

If we desire to magnify the Lord, following the example of Mary, Mother of God, we work for a complete and unconstrained relationship with God. Part of that relationship is a free gift of grace and mercy from God, but the other aspect is our own practice of virtue. We take up the greatest commandments to love God above everything and to love our neighbors as ourselves. The desire to be a Saint demands we foster relationships with people rather than things, achievements, and self-love. We must even give up our ideas of what holiness looks like and seek only God's perfect will for us as His daughters.

We simply can't magnify the Lord without being a martyr in some sense. In some parts of the world, people are physically dying in the name of Christ; but no matter where we live, God asks us to die to our selfish ambition and desires. He invites us to follow His example of the cross as the ultimate image of love. The meaning of magnifying the Lord will be as unique to each of us as our own souls. The Magnify meditations will help us to pray and discern, and then live out the specific ways that God calls us to enflame our sphere of influence.

We must be concerned with our own interior lives. We deepen our spirituality by growing in virtue so that we can recognize God's grace as it moves in our souls. Then we can magnify His Truth, Goodness, and Beauty.

It isn't easy living a radical and authentically Christian life. How do we avoid compromising the Truth in an age where tolerance seems to mean relativism and blatant disregard for moral truth? How do we invite others to a life of genuine love when they don't even know they want it, because love seems to mean "do what makes you happy"?

We are called to go out into the world and be the witnesses of the Good News (see Mark 16:15). Are we willing to "die" for our love of God? Is He increasing as we decrease? Do our souls proclaim His greatness by the way we live our lives?

How do we detach from the worldly culture so that we can feel true freedom as disciples of Jesus? It's a daunting task, especially in the global materialistic society of today. Our incarnate bodies are created to experience God through our senses, and everything God made is good! Yet, we've too often made worldly comfort and things an idol, not as the means to draw closer to God's ultimate Goodness. Our "consumerized" senses draw us away from our identity as daughters of God and distract us so much that we stop striving for greatness and settle for material contentment. We fear true intimacy because of past wounds or interior walls we've built through being let down by those around us. We find it so hard to let God love us, because we can't see a visible example of perfect love. We've got to get out of our own way and surrender to Him.

We are tempted by human approval and desire for attention; by security and comfort found in homes, clothes, health, and meals; by beauty's or physique's vanity; by our to-do lists for productivity while maintaining a home, career, or both. We may also be tempted with despair, anxiety, and addictions to things that fill our body or mind yet leave our soul empty. The full Magnify experience contains mortifications to bring these afflictions to the surface, and then meet them head on by letting go of our tight grip of expectations.

This book may be read with no additional life changes; however, it's hard to grow in holiness if nothing in our lives changes. The Catechism of the Catholic Church reminds us that we, like all of creation, are in a constant state of journeying. The decision to journey into the desert of asceticism is one to be prayed about, certainly. The Initiator of our desire for perfect love, the Holy Spirit, will guide our discernment of areas of asceticism. We can trust God. His Good and Perfect Love anchors our soul and the meditations that follow will draw us deeper into His will for our lives. Even if baby-steps are what we start with—we must start! And we must continue.

Many women spend their lives in a cycle of trading a few vices for a few others; giving something up only to replace it with some other distraction, making excuses for why we don't have enough time to pray or serve others, and/or minimizing our baptismal call to holiness by blending into a culture of lukewarmness. We end up settling for living a life less than becoming of a saint, often out of fear. We are afraid of missing some worldly thing or event. We are afraid of judgment from others, from ourselves. We are afraid of intimacy—afraid of people seeing our true broken, wounded self. How frequently we try to hide from God, and even ourselves!

So, even though we may not think we need to, and we definitely don't want to, we must give up a lot of what our senses tell us will fulfill us. As we meditate on virtues and how they pull us deeper into the mystery of our own feminine genius, God can transform our wounds, including our fears, when we tear down all the walls and let our attachments and vices go. Let's stop the stiff-arming and open our souls to wholeness that comes from reliance on the Father's Love and Providence. To grow in virtue, we can never give up leaning into God.

In addition to daily prayer; praise, worship, and adoration of God; and joyfully getting to experience life with less attachments; "Magnify 90" involves cultivating intentional relationships with those around us because virtues naturally flow from our soul into our active life. We build up the Kingdom of God by listening more than we talk, making eye contact and meeting others (rather than staring at our screens), and offering prayers and small sacrifices for people we encounter, even only briefly. Instead of focusing on ourselves and the things we are giving up, we focus on what we are free to do and be.

Living out Magnify in the career / professional life

How can we invite the Lord into the working-in-the-world sphere more?

Prioritizing personal career success to the exclusive of our feminine genius can distract us from our call to holiness. The culture that focuses on individual pride and "self-made" stories needs what fiercely Catholic professional women are: souls that elevate everyone around them to a higher mission. What are those around us seeking in their core being? What is the root of what they are longing for? How can we help others around us see God and support them in becoming attentive to their interior life? We must also be more aware of God working through people and circumstances in our work to deepen our own understanding of Him.

Consider starting an early morning or lunch time bible study with co-workers on- or off-site, invite a new could-be-friend to lunch instead of the same go-to group, extend a listening ear to a struggling co-worker rather than exchanging just pleasantries, find common ground with people who can be challenging, pray for peace with someone who causes injuries. Invite fallen away Catholic co-workers to dinner to build a relationship and witness to what joy there is in Christ; utilize a discreet religious item in an office or cubicle—such as placing a bible on a bookshelf—to keep the faith conversation doors open.

Living to Magnify in the unpaid life

How can we invite the Lord into the work we do in our homes?

It can seem as if there is no glory being in the trenches of life as a student, child rearing and homemaking, caring for aging parents, or anything that isn't paid work; so we want recognition from others and pride in ourselves from something. We may be tempted to look to our body or material output for our worth. Society tells us self-care is eating perfectly planned meals that are picture-worthy, working out daily and hitting a personal best on the course, or ladies' nights with some wine-and-whine or a pedicure and massage. This makes us feel refreshed in some ways, but if those things (or similar outlets) are all there is for us regarding weekend goals and recreation, we aren't seeking freedom. Our "self-care" is just enslaving us to more things, achievements, or comfort.

There's nothing inherently wrong with fancy vacations and working out every morning; but if we prioritize those things but alsocan't seem to make time for a Rosary, daily Mass, and/or daily meditation, perhaps our priorities aren't lining up. Nonetheless, this isn't about checking off boxes, it's about ordering our days to live like God is our priority, and everything else is just details. It's recognizing our deep longing for connection with the One who loves us more than we love ourselves. The fact is, making time for prayer and quiet—time for our interior life—is the self-care God asks us to do. We can't love others the way Christ asks us to without His help. Pursuing a relationship with God is the best self-care we could give ourselves; it's soul-care. And when we really invest in that, true joy becomes a reality and not just something we steal little glimpses of here or there.

Consider starting date nights or ladies' nights with adoration of the Blessed Sacrament or confession. Invite friends to your home with their wild brood of kids to socialize, enjoy fellowship, and then pray together amidst the chaos. Ask other couples to start a small group bible study.Check in on the neighbor that lives a life completely different from your own, sharing a meal or tea and ask her how you can pray for her. Find a group in your area that doesn't just give to the poor, but stands in solidarity with them, eating together and building friendships. Linger after Mass to chat with anyone else that's around. Skip the dusting at that exact moment and pray a chaplet of Divine Mercy in the 3 p.m. hour. Hang images of saints in your home. Light candles when you pray a family Rosary. Go to a cafe and pray for each person there as you sip your coffee.

Do the next right thing, start small, pray for guidance. Ask God to remove the desire for self-fulfillment and human respect. Once we have our identity resting in God alone, our mission becomes easier to realize: we are all called to be Saints. As feminine geniuses, we shift our focus from what do I want, what am I getting, to I do what God wants.
It's worth noting that we will inevitably fall short, but it is a daily choice to start renewed by His mercy. May our journey here lead us closer to God. And I am sure that he who began a good work in you will bring it to completion at the day of Jesus Christ. (Philippians 1:6 NRSV-CE). Sisters, I look forward to seeing the light of Christ magnified in each one of you—I know it will set the world on fire with love.

Your Why for Magnify

Take some time to pray and consider the following: "Why am I entering into this time of intentional prayer and sacrifice? What are my intentions?" Use the space below to record your why.

_____

_____

_____

_____

_____

_____

_____

_____

_____

_____

_____

_____

_____

_____

_____

_____

MAGNIFY 90 GUIDELINES

Discussion with a spiritual director, priest, or mentor is suggested, but ultimately prayer before the Blessed Sacrament is the best way to discern what God is asking you to take up and give up.

Sundays and Solemnities may be lesser in self-denial. If there is a major life or sacramental celebration during the 90 days, prayerfully discern if God is asking you to take a brief reprieve or small allowance from your planned-out mortifications to be unified in celebrating with others. Praise of God is higher than any sacrifice we could offer.

- Daily prayer of at least 30 minutes, including:
  - Mary's Magnificat (Luke 1:46-55)
  - Litany of Humility alternated with Litany of Trust
  - Rosary; mysteries, scriptural, or meditative
- Frequent sacraments: monthly confession, daily Mass, as best as state in life allows
- Weekly scheduled adoration, if no perpetual adoration exists in your area, prayer before the tabernacle is great.
- Listen to only uplifting Christian or classical music. Podcasts should only be ones that challenge you to higher virtue. If in doubt, choose silence.
- No TV/videos except religious programming in moderation (such as formed.org)
- Identify a person daily to offer your mortification for and pray for this person by name.
- Go out of your way to contact people that come to mind in prayer time, God brought them to mind for a reason.
- Go for intentional walks with your friend or husband—Jesus was always walking with others
- There should be no weighing on the scale. (Unless this is required by a doctor) -- When we weigh ourselves, with no true medical need, we are yet again chaining ourselves to attachments of this world. There may also be a temptation to see the Magnify 90 fasts as a way to lose weight…of course this wouldn't be our motivation, but it could be seen as a silver lining. This is not what we want to have tempting us in the back of our mind! Stay off the scale.
- Don't consume sweets and alcohol, and don't snack between meals.
- Participate in no social media (discern if necessary for your job on a professional level)

MAGNIFY 90 GUIDELINES

- Avoid non-essential purchases, stick to food and toiletries, no home goods/shoes/clothes/etc that arent absolutely essential, basically no unnecessary shopping (if you are married, discuss this with your husband for his agreement) because if you cut out media and shows, you may be tempted to browse online shopping as a distraction from prayer and real life

- Fridays are a day of meatless fasting (2 smaller meals)

- No make-up worn on Wednesday + Friday, traditional days of fasting, simple appearance other days: minimal accessories/make up — a step in the reclaiming of a Christian culture. In our deep heart of hearts, most of us will admit we wear it because we feel like our face isnt enough, because we want people to like the way we look, or even just because everyone else does it--so we will stand out and look somehow "less" if we dont. But this desert is about stripping things away, so that our faith in God is what we cling to. Yes, it may seem hard and scary...so let us look to the modest appearance of Saints and religious sisters as examples of Christian joy being the "make-up" we wear. Make-up isnt necessary for femininity. You may certainly opt to avoid make up completely.

MATERNITY MAGNIFY 90 GUIDELINES

The Maternity Magnify 90 will allow prenatal and postnatal mothers to practice mortification within their state in life, while drawing nearer to Mary, the Mother of God as they seek to magnify the Lord.

Although both of them together are parents of their child, the woman's motherhood constitutes a special "part" in this shared parenthood, and the most demanding part. Parenthood - even though it belongs to both - is realized much more fully in the woman, especially in the prenatal period. It is the woman who "pays" directly for this shared generation, which literally absorbs the energies of her body and soul. It is therefore necessary that the man be fully aware that in their shared parenthood he owes a special debt to the woman. – Pope St. John Paul II (MD 18)

Maternity Magnify 90 sojourners follow the same Magnify 90 program with the following modifications:

- Remove the snacking restriction. Instead, add no creamers, honey, etc. to your drinks for the entire program.

- The Friday Fast maintains no meat, but does not limit snacks or meal size/frequency at all! Eat to satiation while still fasting from meat. Protein can certainly come from nuts, beans, eggs, etc...for that one day. The suggested Maternity Magnify 90 Friday mortification is no radio/music/programing (not even religious).

For participating expectant mommas suffering from "insomnia," rather than browse the internet, have extra prayer time and include a journaling session to record prayers/thoughts for upcoming baby and even daddy--this will certainly be a treasured time for God to speak life beyond exhaustion.

- Get a notebook and each night that you find sleep difficult, write down letters to baby...how you met his or her dad, stories of your own childhood, how you came to know Jesus, what inspires baby's name, what hopes and dreams you have for baby... Things that come to mind can be turned into part of your day time prayer the next day! Reflect on gratitude! ***Not obsessing over things on the internet or scrolling social media may even improve your mood.

MATERNITY MAGNIFY 90 GUIDELINES

While life is busy and hectic as a prenatal/postnatal mom, strive to still pray a daily rosary, especially try to do this with your children, or over your children, if they are too small. More graces than you realize come from this devotion. It may look externally irreverent with kids flailing about, but your internal reverence is what's key! Stay peaceful, even if you need to correct children's behavior at times.

*** Seek medical advice from a doctor only, follow your care provider's recommendations during pregnancy and the postnatal time, Maternity Magnify mortifications should never risk the health of mother and baby ***

PRAYER INTENTIONS

Use this space to make a list of who or what you are offering your intentions for each day of Magnify 90.

1 _____

2 _____

3 _____

4 _____

5 _____

6 _____

7 _____

8 _____

9 _____

10 _____

11 _____

12 _____

13 _____

14 _____

15 _____

16 _____

17 _____

18 _____

19 _____

20 _____

21 _____

22 _____

23 _____

24 _____

25 _____

26 _____

27 _____

28 _____

29 _____

30 _____

31 _____

32 _____

33 _____

34 _____

35 _____

36 _____

37 _____

38 _____

39 _____

40 _____

41 _____

42 _____

43 _____

44 _____

45 _____

46 _____

PRAYER INTENTIONS

Use this space to make a list of who or what you are offering your intentions for each day of Magnify 90.

47 _____

48 _____

49 _____

50 _____

51 _____

52 _____

53 _____

54 _____

55 _____

56 _____

57 _____

58 _____

59 _____

60 _____

61 _____

62 _____

63 _____

64 _____

65 _____

66 _____

67 _____

68 _____

69 _____

70 _____

71 _____

72 _____

73 _____

74 _____

75 _____

76 _____

77 _____

78 _____

79 _____

80 _____

81 _____

82 _____

83 _____

84 _____

85 _____

86 _____

87 _____

88 _____

89 _____

90 _____

Humility

St. Gemma Galgani

WEEK 1 - HUMILITY
St. Gemma Galgani

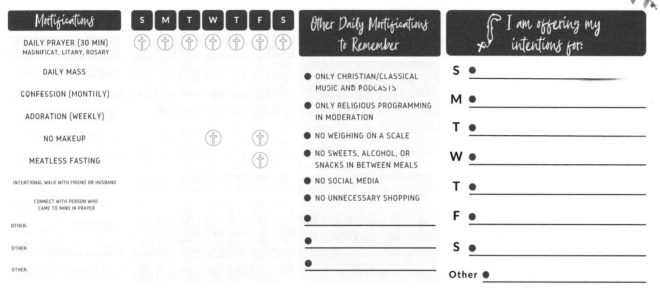

Mortifications	S	M	T	W	T	F	S
DAILY PRAYER (30 MIN) MAGNIFICAT, LITANY, ROSARY	✝	✝	✝	✝	✝	✝	✝
DAILY MASS							
CONFESSION (MONTHLY)							
ADORATION (WEEKLY)							
NO MAKEUP			✝		✝		
MEATLESS FASTING					✝		
INTENTIONAL WALK WITH FRIEND OR HUSBAND							
CONNECT WITH PERSON WHO CAME TO MIND IN PRAYER							
OTHER:							
OTHER:							
OTHER:							

Other Daily Mortifications to Remember

- ONLY CHRISTIAN/CLASSICAL MUSIC AND PODCASTS
- ONLY RELIGIOUS PROGRAMMING IN MODERATION
- NO WEIGHING ON A SCALE
- NO SWEETS, ALCOHOL, OR SNACKS IN BETWEEN MEALS
- NO SOCIAL MEDIA
- NO UNNECESSARY SHOPPING
- _____
- _____
- _____

I am offering my intentions for:

S ● _____
M ● _____
T ● _____
W ● _____
T ● _____
F ● _____
S ● _____
Other ● _____

Express

Use this space to journal, draw, or otherwise express your thoughts on this week's virtue. Spend some time listening to the Holy Spirit, perhaps in Adoration, and capture whatever He brings to mind or lays on your heart.

HUMILITY: DAY 1

We are invited to draw near to Christ own example of self denial so that we may grow in holiness. Our souls, prompted by the Holy Spirit, let us to this desert-amidst-the-world journey to find peace and joy.

Catechism of the Catholic Church § 2015 The way of perfection passes by way of the Cross. There is no holiness without renunciation and spiritual battle. (see 2 Tim. 4) spiritual progress entails the ascesis and mortification that gradually lead to living in the peace and joy of the Beatitudes: "He who climbs never stops going from beginning to beginning, through beginnings that have no end. He never stops desiring what he already knows." (St. Gregory of Nyssa)

Driven by human success through individualism, we find ourselves hiding behind a false idea of freedom. The devil is very crafty as he tempts those seeking holiness away from the source of Truth and all Goodness. Pride worms its way into our life, often when we don't even notice it. We want to do what we want to do, when we want to do it, rather than striving toward freedom from sin and attachment. We become subtly convinced it's better to avoid the cross of suffering and mortification. Self-loving pride tells us the truth can't really be defined and that we are better off trusting only ourselves.

Or presumptive pride convinces us to make a list of tasks that we can check off and know beyond a shadow of a doubt that we are going to Heaven when we die. We compare ourselves to others and consider ourselves "good people." Pride convinces us that we can earn Heaven. Yet we harden our hearts to the crosses God uses to draw us closer to Him. We want to cultivate our own parameters for being Christian, rather than diving deep into the wounds of Christ where only sacrificial love remains. Perhaps, on the other hand, we struggle with reverse pride: neglecting to acknowledge we are beloved by God. We dismiss the gifts God gives us each day and instead, dwell in places of fear, worry, anxiety, and isolation. We get into a deep depression, considering ourselves unworthy of authentic love. We rely on coping mechanisms: wine, food, gossip, binge-watching TV, obsession with fitness/vanity, seeking reassurance from others, etc… anything to numb the pain of feeling empty. This is actually prideful too, thinking we know better than God who made us in His image!

Christian humility is not self-deprecating, it is recognizing that we are not gods. Humility gives us the rightly ordered relationship with our Trinitarian God. We recognize our need for God's grace and allow it to permeate our open hearts—not ones closed off by selfish ambition or blocked by worldly consumption. Humility is found in trusting God rather than seeking worldly security.

We each bring unique desires to this journey, but our goal is the same: to become the saints God created us to be. To go into spiritual battle against our attachments—material or mental—we must rid ourselves of pride and renounce our vices. Humility lets us admit we need help. We need the graces in the Sacraments, we need time reading the Bible, and we need to foster intentional relationships not built around appearances, media, or gossip. With humility as our starting point, we begin to drown out the culture that encourages us to suppress the longing for God by filling our life with anything other than God.

 **Take time to honestly assess specific areas of pride (and reverse pride) in your life. How does that affect your ability to be open to spiritual growth? How can you better invite Christ to be what fills you? Where is He inviting you to trust Him more?**

HUMILITY: DAY 2

Committing to asceticism and a deep prayer life is very counter cultural, and only by the grace of God are we able to join our will and our strength with His. St. Gemma Galgani had ecstasies of conversations with Jesus about suffering, love, and the cross. She is a feminine genius example of humility.

"I hoped, oh Jesus, as I confessed so many times before you, to be self-sufficient in something; I hoped in my own strength... But when I began to act on my own, that was when I fell and lost all you had allowed me to gain. But soon after, oh Jesus, you illuminated me, and then I understood that what I thought I could be self-sufficient in was exactly what I never could have done on my own. I had the will but lacked strength; I had the strength but lacked the will...Before you I have absolutely nothing to boast about!" *– St. Gemma Galgani (Rudolph M. Bell, Saint Gemma Galgani, Cristina Mazzoni. The Voices of Gemma Galgani: The Life and Afterlife of a Modern Saint (2003) Univ. of Chicago Press)*

Humble yourselves therefore under the mighty hand of God, that in due time he may exalt you. Cast all your anxieties on him, for he cares about you. Be sober, be watchful. Your adversary the devil prowls around like a roaring lion, seeking someone to devour. Resist him, firm in your faith, knowing that the same experience of suffering is required of your brotherhood throughout the world. And after you have suffered a little while, the God of all grace, who has called you to his eternal glory in Christ, will himself restore, establish, and strengthen you. *– 1 Peter 5:6-10*

Temptation to feel pride can easily spoil the effects that true asceticism is meant to give us: a deeper relationship with God. We cannot let Magnify 90 be a prideful endeavor—it should remind us how far we still have to go in our journey and inspire us to press forward! Magnifying the Lord is only possible when we are humble like our Blessed Mother, Mary. She was conceived without sin, and humbly aligned her will with God's, accepting sorrows as part of her Fiat, knowing that He would be her strength. So then shouldn't we, as sinners, foster humility by accepting the crosses in our lives?

Holiness is never obtained through our own doing, so by recognizing all good things are from God, we can keep our pride in check. Magnify 90 is not meant to be a public display of mortification. In fact, we should discern whom to speak with about it, so as not to cause ourselves or others to fall into further sin. We aren't doing this for human recognition, but if we start living more joyful lives, simpler and peaceful lives, there will be opportunities to share the cause of our joy—the freedom found in living for the Lord!

Sisters, as we strive to grow closer to Him, the devil will try to derail us. If we see temptations as an opportunity to rely on the Lord even more deeply, our humility grows. We know that God never forsakes us, so we can stay close to Him in prayer, confident that His greater glory will always triumph.

Consider When have you had the strength to do something but not the will power, or the will but not the strength? Have you thought you could handle something, without really taking it to prayer, only to later realize it was God all along? How does staying close to Jesus, casting all your worries on God, make you able to resist temptations to be self-sufficient?

HUMILITY: DAY 3

Picking up our crosses to follow Christ daily is necessary to fully live a Christian life. The cross is our magnifying glass for humility and love.

CCC 618: The cross is the unique sacrifice of Christ, the "one mediator between God and men." (1 Timothy 2:5) But because in his incarnate divine person he has in some way united himself to every man, "the possibility of being made partners, in a way known to God, in the paschal mystery" is offered to all men. (Gaudium et Spes 22 § 5, see also § 2) He calls his disciples to "take up [their] cross and follow [him] (Matthew 16:24)," for "Christ also suffered for [us], leaving [us] an example so that [we] should follow in his steps (1 Peter 2:21)". In fact Jesus desires to associate with his redeeming sacrifice those who were to be its first beneficiaries. This is achieved supremely in the case of his mother, who was associated more intimately than any other person in the mystery of his redemptive suffering. (see Luke 2:35) "Apart from the cross there is no other ladder by which we may get to heaven." (St. Rose of Lima)

During Magnify 90 we choose to forgo certain comforts, such as make-up, snacking, desserts, and shopping for non-essentials. We do this to detach from things that get in the way of our prayer life, things that cause us distraction from being attached only to God. They aren't necessarily bad, they just aren't encouraging us to rely fully on a relationship with God. If we can't give them up for a few months, perhaps we are more attached to them than we'd like to believe. All gifts from God must be rightly ordered. Denying our desire for comforts over the next few months will help us see more clearly the will of God in our life.

These little voluntary mortifications are ways that we strengthen our ability to carry the involuntary crosses that may come our way. When we practice virtue in small things—such as being unattached to physical beauty or a nightly drink—we are more aware of our need for God's grace to lead us through the physical, emotional, or spiritual hardships that we do not want and can't change.

We practice humility each time we want to watch a trashy TV show but realize what we actually crave is human connection, so we call a loved one or invite friends over to have good conversation. Our humility grows each time we want to distract ourselves by snacking on chocolate but turn toward prayer instead. Staying off social media keeps us humble because we aren't tempted to compare our lives to others, we are less tempted to gossip, and we recognize that Jesus wants us to be present with those around us in real life.

Humility is looking for the goodness of God in others, knowing they are carrying a longing as well. We can magnify the Lord to them by offering solidarity, prayers, and friendship. As we strive to think of others' needs more than our own, we will find that we are loving like Christ loves. We are joining Him in suffering as co-redeemers. We are living as conduits for the love of Christ to permeate the world.

Consider

How do daily mortifications help strengthen your relationship with God? How does humility help you avoid looking at ascetism as something to "be good at"? What specific connections do you see in your own life between suffering, humility, and trust? Consider adding the song "Magnify" by We Are Messengers as part of your prayer today.

HUMILITY: DAY 4

The way in which we accept our cross gives hope to others, helps us live joyfully; but most importantly helps us to be united to Christ.

"My daughter, if the Cross was not felt, it could not be called a Cross. Be certain that if you stand beneath the Cross you will never be lost. The Devil has no power over those souls who weep near the Cross. My daughter, how many would have abandoned Me, if I had not crucified them. The Cross is a very precious gift, and many virtues can be learned through it." – *Jesus to St. Gemma Galgani (Father Amedeo, C.P. Blessed Gemma Galgani (1878-1903) (1935) Burns, Oates, and Washbourne, London)*

"My child, you complain because I will to keep thee in the dark; but remember that after darkness comes light, and then you shalt have light indeed. I put thee to this test for My greater glory, to give joy to the angels, for thy greater gain, and also for example to others. ...Though it seems to thee that I repel thee, know that instead I draw thee more closely to Myself....Think only for the present of how you are to practice great virtue; make haste in the ways of divine love, humble thyself, and rest assured that if I keep thee on the Cross, I love thee." – *Jesus to St. Gemma Galgani (Venerable Reverend Germanus C.P. The Life of St. Gemma Galgani (2014) Catholic Way Publishing)*

St. Gemma's spirituality revolved around humility. She recognized everything as a gift from God, a grace in her life necessary to make her a saint. Despite intense suffering, she found joy in the love of Christ.

There are four levels of happiness that philosophers discuss. The first involves bodily pleasures to fulfill a physical happiness search, and the second involves comparing ourselves to others to find relative happiness. The third is the happiness we feel when we help others, and the fourth is called transcendent, a happiness found beyond ourselves.

Transcendent happiness isn't found in wanting what others have, or obsession with some pleasure-inducing comfort. When we find ourselves concerned with keeping up with what the neighbors have or what our social media friends do, we can't feel fully happy because there will always be something more to consume or more to do. Transcendent happiness is found in God. It is found in freedom from attachments that consume our mind and energy. The Christian life is a beautiful full effort of loving God both transcendently and tangibly in our neighbor; so we keep a loop between the third and fourth levels of happiness. Unshakeable joy is found in freedom from needing to numb emotions and freedom from enslaving our bodies to comfort. It is found in breaking the chains of obsession with power, money, and "stuff." When we can say no to something the world offers, then we are free. True peace of spirit is found when having or not having doesn't affect our soul.

No matter what suffering we are going through, happiness that's found in God can never go away. All around us are involuntary crosses like cancer, infertility, or unemployment; perhaps we are carrying these burdens ourselves. As Jesus told St. Gemma, these are a gift—though they certainly don't feel like it! These crosses seem like a tragic, dark, isolating loneliness. Humility helps us know that even if we can't see a positive outcome, we trust that God has our greater good beyond these crosses. He is trustworthy because He created us for Good, died on the cross for us despite our denial of His Lordship, and is always inviting us into an eternity of joy. We have a God that loves us so much He came to earth to show us what true love looks like so that we can share in His Divine life.

What things in life are you clinging too tightly to? What is keeping you from unshakeable joy? Do you hold any expectations about fairness or other comparison measures that inhibit your humility? When have you experienced transcendent happiness, as a foretaste to Heaven?

HUMILITY: DAY 5

Humility is irrelevant without faith, and faith requires active participation; we can't just sit by and let life happen. We must seek out opportunities for God's grace to permeate our lives. We have to live our lives ruled by our belief in God and our assent to His Truth.

"And without faith it is impossible to please him. For whoever would draw near to God must believe that he exists and that he rewards those who seek him. – *Hebrews 11:6*

Now great multitudes accompanied him; and he turned and said to them, "If anyone comes to me and does not hate his own father and mother and wife and children and brothers and sisters, yes, and even his own life, he cannot be my disciple. Whoever does not bear his own cross and come after me, cannot be my disciple. For which of you, desiring to build a tower, does not first sit down and count the cost, whether he has enough to complete it? Otherwise, when he has laid a foundation, and is not able to finish, all who see it begin to mock him, saying, 'This man began to build, and was not able to finish.' – *Luke 14:25-30*

How can we possibly become Saints if our resources—material and mental—are spent on building up worldly fortunes or statuses. If our lifestyles revolve around consumerism and secular activities, we disrupt our ability to prioritize prayer, the sacraments, and helping others see the face of Christ. Taking an honest assessment of what we are good at doing: engineering, painting, listening, building, baking, organizing, hosting, encouraging, teaching, planning, etc.…, then using these gifts for the benefit of others' journeys toward God is to recognize our place within the big picture of salvation history. Humility is planting seeds and being unattached to seeing them grow, or even harvested.

The following quote has been attributed to St. Teresa of Avila, "Christ has no body now but yours; no hands, no feet on earth but yours…" but it's not found in any of her writings or teachings; it actually comes from Protestant writings (The British Friend vol 1, no 1, 1892 pg. 15) combined into a poem. Additionally, it isn't even true theologically, given that the Eucharist is the True Body and Blood of Christ on Earth. The humble sentiment is to think of offering our hands and feet to do God's will, our bodies as belonging to Him via the Church, His Bride. Our faith compels us to let Jesus' love flow out from us to others as we bear His Light through building relationships and praising God. Faith isn't something we are able to give, it's our own deeply personal experience that we live out so that others are inspired to tap into their own gift of faith from God.

We can still own a home and car, we still work in the secular environment, we can still enjoy good food and drink, we can play sports and watch movies… but these things must be rightly ordered. We use them to experience the Divine as He intended creation to be thoughtfully enjoyed and savored (not mindlessly consumed and taken for granted or put upon a pedestal as an idol through the way we prioritize our time). Each person must maintain human dignity in the world. Humility in our vocation is about using the gifts God has given us to care about the good of others. We can utilize things and activities to offer hospitality, support, and consolation. This brings us great joy because we draw nearer to God every time we seek Him in others.

Consider

How have you experienced joy this week? Perhaps you've been surprised that your suffering was turned into joy...or your mortifications made a way for you to experience a joyful moment more deeply? How do you continue to grow in your faith? How does your life indicate your priorities?

HUMILITY: DAY 6

Humility enhances trust, gratitude, modesty, friendliness…many other virtues are able to flourish when we start on the base level of humility before God.

Gemma, when on her deathbed, being asked by one of the Sisters in attendance what virtue was most important and dearest to God, answered with great vivacity of spirit, "Humility, humility, the foundation of all the others." *(Ven. Father Germanus. The Life of St. Gemma Galgani (2004) Tan Books)*

Or do you suppose it is in vain that the scripture says, "He yearns jealously over the spirit which he has made to dwell in us"? But he gives more grace; therefore it says, "God opposes the proud, but gives grace to the humble."
– James 4:5-6

The most important virtues are the theological ones of faith, hope, and love; which are directed to God. Our human virtue of humility helps us to be receptive to those by setting our disposition to a state of openness to God. All virtues are tied together, and we must grow in them all to become holy. Growing in virtue requires an undoing of learned behaviors that make most of us look out for ourselves above all else.

God gave us a spirit that longs for Him, yet we often use that spirit to pursue so many other distractions. Many humans have a fallen idea and way of living that surviving on the earth is the goal of life, but then faith directs us to see eternal life as much more important. He desires us, He yearns for us—but He doesn't force us to love Him back. If we humble our spirit enough to see His Goodness, we find that He has always been there pouring out grace. As St. Gemma exemplifies for us, humility can be the foundation for all the other virtues.

To live humbly is to be so open to His Will that every day of our life is an adventure of saying yes to love, yes to simplicity, and yes to courageous vulnerability. The relational aspect of humility provides opportunities to be the loved and the lover. If we all care for others as God cares for us, no one wants for anything and joy abounds all the much more. Of course, sin still exists and none of us are perfect, so we keep pursuing holiness and trusting in God's agape love—which is where mercy and forgiveness are conceived. We won't be judged on what we have, but on what we have and give. Practicing humility will enable us to see what gifts and talents God has given us, and then turn around to use them for the good of the whole world. We give all praise to God from whom all goodness flows.

Humility sounds like:
The Lord can do amazing things through me, because He gave me the grace to be receptive to His will.
I don't have enough food, and I offer that up as my cross of loving sacrifice today.
I've been shown mercy, and I share that.
I have faith, and I use that to magnify the Lord.
I have poverty and I invite you into it.
I have time, I want to share it with you.

I have life and I offer it to the next generation.
I have a home, you are welcome here.
I have poverty and I invite you into it.
I have time, I want to share it with you.

Because virtue also recognizes the dignity of others, no matter the worldly status they have or don't have, it also sounds like, *What a blessing you are in my life; I am so glad that God has given (skill, virtue, openness) to you!*

How does humility affect your faith and trust in God? Your personal hope? Why does humility affect the way you love others? What actions in your life are driven by fear of being ridiculed or rejected? Can you find a way to extend dignity to someone you encounter today, in an unexpected way?

HUMILITY: DAY 7

It is impossible to get to Heaven clinging to belongings and status, to our own selfish pride, to our sense of entitlement, or our tight grip on self-reliance. Humility helps us rely on Jesus, which is necessary to be a saint.

CCC 2544: Jesus enjoins his disciples to prefer him to everything and everyone, and bids them "renounce all that [they have]" for his sake and that of the Gospel. (see Luke 14:33) Shortly before his passion he gave them the example of the poor widow of Jerusalem who, out of her poverty, gave all that she had to live on. (see Luke 21:4) The precept of detachment from riches is obligatory for entrance into the Kingdom of heaven.

2545: All Christ's faithful are to "direct their affections rightly, lest they be hindered in their pursuit of perfect charity by the use of worldly things and by an adherence to riches which is contrary to the spirit of evangelical poverty." *(Lumen Gentium 42 § 3)*

We all want to be saints; we want to spend eternity glorifying God in Heaven. But living in the world is so hard—how can we not get swept away with thinking about wanting others to like us or wanting to be needed? We want others to visit our home or office and be impressed. We want others to see we are doing well financially. We want others to know what our talents are. Maybe, in a peculiarly modern way, we also want others to see our cultivated messes to know that we don't think too much of ourselves, while at the same time desiring a ton of social media likes for such "honesty." How many of us struggle with narcissism even if we don't want to?

Magnify 90 involves inward mortifications so that externally we can be free to magnify the Lord. We must prefer Jesus to everything else and we can't point others to Him if we are too distracted. We have so many worries and anxieties in our modern age, and it really stems from a lack of trust. We aren't humbling ourselves enough to admit that God's way is better than our way. We must spend time in silence, listening for the Holy Spirit's guidance.

We pull back the curtains on our brokenness during Magnify 90, to see the places we keep hidden even from ourselves. In practicing humility, we discover our own selfish tendencies, the preferences we have toward body image, the negative attitudes we hold toward those not like us, and the longing we have for real and vulnerable connection. We are free to develop a deeper relationship with Jesus in frequent prayer, we're free to cultivate friendships the Holy Spirit sends our way, and we're free to experience life with grateful hearts. We are free to welcome even suffering as a grace.

Consider

In what areas of life do you crave human acceptance most? How do you live evangelical poverty—that is, in what ways do you live like God is your only treasure? How do you view charity? Is it a box to check or something more? Consider adding "A Future Not My Own" by Matt Maher to your prayer today.

WEEKLY REFLECTIONS

Affability

St. Angela Merici

WEEK 2-AFFABILITY
St. Angela Merici

Mortifications	S	M	T	W	T	F	S	Other Daily Mortifications to Remember	I am offering my intentions for:
DAILY PRAYER (30 MIN) MAGNIFICAT, LITANY, ROSARY	✝	✝	✝	✝	✝	✝	✝		
DAILY MASS								● ONLY CHRISTIAN/CLASSICAL MUSIC AND PODCASTS	S ● _____
CONFESSION (MONTHLY)								● ONLY RELIGIOUS PROGRAMMING IN MODERATION	M ● _____
ADORATION (WEEKLY)								● NO WEIGHING ON A SCALE	T ● _____
NO MAKEUP			✝		✝			● NO SWEETS, ALCOHOL, OR SNACKS IN BETWEEN MEALS	W ● _____
MEATLESS FASTING					✝			● NO SOCIAL MEDIA	T ● _____
INTENTIONAL WALK WITH FRIEND OR HUSBAND								● NO UNNECESSARY SHOPPING	F ● _____
CONNECT WITH PERSON WHO CAME TO MIND IN PRAYER								● _____	S ● _____
OTHER:								● _____	Other ● _____
OTHER:								● _____	
OTHER:									

Express Use this space to journal, draw, or otherwise express your thoughts on this week's virtue. Spend some time listening to the Holy Spirit, perhaps in Adoration, and capture whatever He brings to mind or lays on your heart.

AFFABILITY: DAY 8

Affability invites us to avoid both giving inflated praise and exhibiting grouchiness. This requires us to translate the theological virtue of charity (love for God) into our dealings with others (love for neighbor). To magnify the Lord, we love others as God loves us and overcome attachments to preferences or personal moods.

CCC 1878: All men are called to the same end: God himself. There is a certain resemblance between the unity of the divine persons and the fraternity that men are to establish among themselves in truth and love. *(Gaudium et Spes 24 § 3)* Love of neighbor is inseparable from love for God.

May the God of steadfastness and encouragement grant you to live in such harmony with one another, in accord with Christ Jesus, that together you may with one voice glorify the God and Father of our Lord Jesus Christ. *– Romans 15:5-6*

Make yourself beloved in the congregation…*– Sirach 4:7 (in some translations, beloved is "affable")*

The varied ideas of love, especially in today's age, obscure the reality of what it means to be loving, let alone friendly. Making others feel validated at any cost is not friendly, it's flattery. Excusing sin through relativism is not loving, but neither is having a "holier-than-thou" attitude. There is a need to walk alongside our neighbors—no matter how far from God they may seem to us—because we need others to walk alongside us as well. We need each other on our journeys. Our week meditating on humility led us to understand it's impossible to love others the way God loves them through an act of our will alone. No one can love with a Divine Love without grace, through which we can try to emulate Jesus Christ's sacrificial love.

This time spent in the "desert" is an internal one, not an external one. We are still called to be friendly and involved with others. As grace transforms our self-centered will, we can radiate a joyful attitude and bear the light of Christ to those around us. Let us not be scared to be intentional and authentic with those God puts in our lives. The point of Magnify is to help us love more, to will the good of others more—offering our mortifications each day for a specific intention while being detached from seeing or feeling fruitfulness.

We sever grace in our souls the second we begin to calculate how good we are doing in our ascetic lifestyle and pride creeps back into our life. May we never turn a blind eye to anyone by our own inward focus that leads to sin.

We are called to rise above our attachments, not bemoan them. Giving up our nightly "unwinding" TV time or scrolling through a social media feed is bound, at times, to make us a little grumpy and shorter-tempered with those we live with because we aren't distracting ourselves from real emotions and needs.

Skipping the mimosa with our girlfriends could make us resentful to the point of just not even going out with friends. Yet, we are called to maintain and build friendships! How else would we be able to magnify the Lord to others if we spent our Magnify experience hiding from social interactions? Whatever our most challenging piece of the mortifications are, if we let it cause us to be less affable, we are missing the mark.

Servant of God Chiara Corbella wrote to her son as she was dying: "…Love consumes you, but it is beautiful to die consumed, exactly like a candle that goes out only when it has reached its goal. Anything that you do in life will make sense only if you look at it in view of eternal life. If you are truly loving, you will realize this from the fact that nothing belongs to you, because everything is a gift. As St. Francis says, 'the opposite of love is possession.'" *(Simone Troisi, Christian Paccini, translator Charlotte Fasi. Chiara Corbella Petrillo: A Witness to Joy. Illustrated edition (2015) Sophia Institute Press.)*

how can you stay focused and present with the people right in front of you—thinking not of your to-do list nor of others you'd rather be with. Read all of Romans Chapter 15. Note anything that strikes you from reading this chapter and how it relates to letting love consume you. How do you see a connection between pride, possession-mentality, and distraction within your life?

AFFABILITY: DAY 9

St. Angela Merici was a conduit for the Holy Spirit and a feminine genius of affability. She encouraged women to find holiness in their vocation, to utilize their state in life as an opportunity to be sanctified by grace, and to bring other women to God as well. She wrote often about the virtue of affability, especially within the context of evangelization.

"…let their conversation be instructive and courteous, not harsh or rude, but gentle and peace-loving and charitable. Tell them, that it is my wish, wherever they happen to be, that they should give good example, charming all by the sweet odor of their virtues, showing obedience and submission to all who have authority over them, and zealous to promote good feeling and peace everywhere. Above all, let them be humble and affable, and let holy charity regulate their whole bearing, their every action and word, and let them bear everything patiently..." – *St. Angela Merici (Bernard O'Reilly. St. Angela Merici, and the Ursulines (1880) Pollard & Moss)*

Bless those who persecute you; bless and do not curse them. Rejoice with those who rejoice, weep with those who weep. Live in harmony with one another; do not be haughty, but associate with the lowly; never be conceited. Repay no one evil for evil, but take thought for what is noble in the sight of all. If possible, so far as it depends upon you, live peaceably with all. Beloved, never avenge yourselves, but leave it to the wrath of God; for it is written, "Vengeance is mine, I will repay, says the Lord." No, "if your enemy is hungry, feed him; if he is thirsty, give him drink; for by so doing you will heap burning coals upon his head." Do not be overcome by evil, but overcome evil with good. – *Romans 12:14-21*

CCC 1879 The human person needs to live in society. Society is not for him an extraneous addition but a requirement of his nature. Through the exchange with others, mutual service and dialogue with his brethren, man develops his potential; he thus responds to his vocation. *(Gaudium et Spes 25 § 1)*

Christianity is about relationship, no matter our vocation or state in life. We cannot build up the Kingdom of God if we are isolationists or independent minded. During Magnify, we recollect that things don't matter—people matter. Being affable isn't just surface level. Women have a unique genius—the genius of maternity. Whether we actually give birth to a human life or not, we are called to bring forth His Divine Life into the world over and over again. Following our Blessed Mother Mary and St. Angela Merici (mother to her religious order) this week, we are called to be spiritual mothers through our own "yes" to virtue. We can't stop at just seeking a deeper relationship with God; because He created us for each other too, we live to share His goodness!

The deeper we seek God by cutting out worldly attachments, the more we are free to cooperate with His most perfect will. Relationship with Him, prayer, is how we come to know that will, and it's going to lead to external action. Jesus does not tell His disciples to just think—He commissions them to go out, to make Him known to the world! This is our call too. In our day-to-day living, others must see Christ naturally reflected in us. We've heard it said that arguments don't convert souls, and it's anecdotally true. Vengeance is reserved for the Lord because He is the only one perfect enough to exact it fairly. We've all sinned; we've all fallen short—so the virtuous thing to do is walk charitably and patiently with others. We speak truth in compassionate ways so to encourage the listener more willing to hear. We can actively encourage those around us by just showing up, consistently being a true friend. We should show love more frequently than we talk about it. The works of mercy are a sure way to convey God's love through being affable.

How has joyful friendliness helped your ability to magnify God in the past? Will you try to make any changes going forward? Is there a girlfriend in your life that you recognize as gifted in the area of affability? What characteristics do you notice? Thank her for her witness.

AFFABILITY: DAY 10

We can be better conduits for God's love when we detach from our expectations of how others should act. It would be easy to let go of control if we were omniscient, if we knew how God's ways would come together in the end. Yet, as beings confined to time and limited knowledge, we struggle against the urge to control.

"For all are what God made them, and you know not what glorious use He may yet make of them. ...Correct your dear ones lovingly, charitably, when you see them falling through human infirmity. Thus, will you continue to prune the vine committed to you by our Lord; leaving the result to Him, who will bide His own time to do wonders for you." – *St. Angela Merici (Bernard O'Reilly. St. Angela Merici, and the Ursulines (1880) Pollard & Moss)*

CCC 1936: On coming into the world, man is not equipped with everything he needs for developing his bodily and spiritual life. He needs others. Differences appear tied to age, physical abilities, intellectual or moral aptitudes, the benefits derived from social commerce, and the distribution of wealth. (see also Gaudium et Spes 29 § 2) The "talents" are not distributed equally. (See Matthew 25: 14-30, Luke 19:27)

1937: These differences belong to God's plan, who wills that each receive what he needs from others, and that those endowed with particular "talents" share the benefits with those who need them. These differences encourage and often oblige persons to practice generosity, kindness, and sharing of goods; they foster the mutual enrichment of cultures [...]

We were made for relationship, by a God of relationship. Welcomed into that relationship through our baptism, we are redeemed by Christ's love for us, which came to be through the love of the Father that bent down to Earth in Christ the Son to satisfy the covenant we were unable to fulfill. Redemption is freely given, and salvation must then be accepted through the way we draw near to God while on Earth. The Holy Spirit poured out to us through the Sacraments and mercy restores our freedom to love, to choose right relationship with our Creator and His creation. We live this out in our interactions with other humans, despite our unique differences and needs.

Perhaps one of the hardest things to detach from is the preference to be around people just like us. It's hard to encounter others with the love of Christ when they make us feel uneasy, when they challenge our beliefs or our lifestyle. Or maybe they just come off as annoying or aren't good at social cues. Maybe they try to commandeer everything for their own glory or blame others for their short-comings. When we look at other people with the eyes of Christ, or search for Christ's light in them, we can see that our own preferences don't matter. If God has placed someone in our lives, it's not a coincidence. As St. Francis de Sales wrote: "One can catch more flies with a spoonful of honey than with a hundred barrels of vinegar." How can we bring God glory through our affability—through our kindness and openness to listen that could lead to mutual trust and shared dignity?

Consider

Have you ever ventured away from your close friends to someone new that seemed a bit lonely? Has someone new tried to encounter you at an event? How does getting out of your "bubble" help you balance having your "cup filled" versus "filling" someone else's? What can we learn about God from others—not theologically, but relationally?

AFFABILITY: DAY 11

If we can deny ourselves human comforts of sweet treats, social media, snacks, make up, shopping—we can deny ourselves selfishness and parameters for who we can befriend. We strive to perfect the virtue of affability so that by getting to know others' hearts, we can speak the words and do the things that will help them—and ourselves—know God better.

CCC 1931: Respect for the human person proceeds by way of respect for the principle that "everyone should look upon his neighbor (without any exception) as 'another self,' above all bearing in mind his life and the means necessary for living it with dignity." (Gaudium et Spes 27 § 1) No legislation could by itself do away with the fears, prejudices, and attitudes of pride and selfishness which obstruct the establishment of truly fraternal societies. Such behavior will cease only through the charity that finds in every man a "neighbor," a brother.

Many people in the world try to fill a God shaped hole with "not-God," and this leads to so much sadness, emptiness, and loneliness. The antidote for that is intimacy. Intimacy in the sense of real human contact, support, and compassion. Of course, it is also intimacy with God, such that we know our dignity and have confidence in His desire for our eternal life. The witness of this to others can be found through us, sisters! God wills to work through us.

Relationships with others are vitally important to the cultural shift we so desire to see. We want evil to disappear, joy to triumph, and peace to reign. God gives us the answer for this explicitly many times in the bible. There's no program that will fix the world. Love is the answer! We must seek to love our fellow humans—all of them. Love wants the eternal good for each person. Yes, the ones who drive us nuts or rub us the wrong way. The ones who have wronged us. The non-Catholic and even anti-Catholic. The ones who very blatantly lead a life of grievous sin. The ones who are invisible and on the fringe of society. The dirty and smelly. The contagiously sick. The ones we can't communicate with easily due to a special need. And of course, the ones who are already dear to us. If we want them all to have eternal happiness, this should affect the way we interact with them, knowing we are modeling Christ to them. Our relationship with God must be deep, and it follows that our relationship with others must be deep.

We must be receptive to those God is already putting in our sphere of influence; we can witness Christian joy through affability with the administrative assistant at work, the barista or waitress, taxi driver, gym attendant, post office worker, the bagger at the store, the neighbor we wave at when getting the mail, an office cube-mate, our kiddo's friends or their parents, our mothers, our daughters-in-law, a godchild; the list is endless. We never know who our next new friend could be, if only we're open to it by being friendly ourselves. People want to be friends with people who are affable, so if God calls us to friendship with a current acquaintance, we can sincerely try to develop one! Yet, we must recognize God created each person with a unique soul, with freedom to deny love. In an offering of love, we can find peace in knowing we've done all we can do if friendship is denied. That's when our mortifications and sacrifices can find deeper meaning.

Mortification shouldn't be viewed as a bad thing. It is a tool that frees us from the bonds of the world's idols. Giving up make-up might be an incredible sacrifice for us, but it can be a helpful exercise in seeing our true God-given beauty. We can come to radiate joy by knowing our happiness isn't based on what other people (or we) see on our skin, but rather on the love of Christ that sustains us. Perhaps we struggle to make mental space for prayer daily—can we take little steps each day? If we begin by saying "yes" to daily prayer, the Lord may open doors for us to humbly accept His invitation to the daily sacrifice of the Mass more frequently. The Eucharist is the source of our strength, so if we find ourselves feeling inadequate in affability—it is a good and virtuous thing to rely on Jesus! Take advantage of the Sacraments to be sustained, especially as we seek to magnify Him.

How has Christ strengthened you in the past, while asking you to be a shoulder to lean on for others (in your family, friends, parish, and community)? Identify someone in your life that you haven't given much attention and consider why. Is God calling you to a deeper love?

AFFABILITY: DAY 12

Humans were created because God is love and so it was necessary, in a way, for someone to exist for which love is directed. There's the need for continued creation through our desire to love and be loved, as we cooperate with God's creative nature. We need each other to be able to live out the greatest commandment.

CCC 1942 The virtue of solidarity goes beyond material goods. In spreading the spiritual goods of the faith, the Church has promoted, and often opened new paths for, the development of temporal goods as well. And so throughout the centuries has the Lord's saying been verified: "Seek first his kingdom and his righteousness, and all these things shall be yours as well" (Matthew 6:33) [...]

"Be pleased to go often … to visit your dear daughters and sisters, and to greet them in all kindness, to see how they are, to comfort them, and to encourage them to persevere in the manner of life they have chosen, to excite a desire of the heavenly joys and possessions, to look longingly forward to the joyous feats and unspeakable delights of the City of God, to its blissful and everlasting triumphs, and to tear themselves away from this love of this pitiful and treacherous world, where no one can find either true rest or contentment, but only empty delusions, bitter labor, and everything miserable and paltry... of this assured prospect let nothing make them doubt, no matter what may be their trouble or difficulty; for all these little miseries will soon vanish from their path, and be succeeded by serenity and joy; and then again, the little we may have to endure in this life is as nothing in comparison to the wealth of happiness stored up in Paradise..." – *St. Angela Merici (Bernard O'Reilly. St. Angela Merici, and the Ursulines (1880) Pollard & Moss)*

Being affable can be thought of as cultivating a sense of solidarity with others. Not only do we have to show love materially (by sharing what resources we have through encountering the poor and having a hospitable culture in our home), we have to show love spiritually. We need each other because we can't do every single thing for ourselves, and we can't follow the Lord's greatest commandment without having neighbors to love! We have to reach out and care about the state of our friends' souls—we have to avoid being overly concerned with ourselves and our own plans and woes. This is spiritual solidarity. We must take care of our own interior life; that's very true, but we also should encourage those around us to find joy in their suffering, to lift their drooping hearts, and to stand steadfast in their vocations. This requires we be good listeners—paying attention to body language and what they don't say, just as much as to what they do say. We pray with and for others, and trust others will do the same for us. No one should be left isolated or wanting in the spiritual life, just as no one should be in the bodily sense either.

If we don't have routine accountability with others, we may find ourselves waking up each day and going about life untethered and distracted, or worse, as if seeking comfort, approval, and independence is all there is to do. We need to remind each other that suffering has a purpose; virtuous growth is more important than comfort, and a committed prayer life is vital to relationship with God. We need others around us that aren't afraid to call us back to the spiritually necessary things—and we can try to be that accountability for others.

Consider How are you encouraging your friends to stand in the truth of their calling to be a saint? Do you lift up and affirm other Christians in a spirit of affability—not giving flattery nor focusing on physical elements? Call a friend today, greet her, ask how she is, listen with your whole heart, then encourage her.

AFFABILITY: DAY 13

To magnify the Lord to those that desperately need to see Him we must tap into affability. We have to find the sweet-spot of not giving into vice because those around us are, yet also not arguing with or ignoring the people of different lifestyles whom God asks us to love.

"Be affable & courteous…You will effect more by loving words, and a courteous manner, than by bitterness, or sharp reprehension, which should never be used but in extreme necessity, and with a prudent regard to the place and time, as well as to the disposition of the person addressed. True charity, which aims in all things to honor God and to be useful to souls, knows how to teach this practical discernment; —it impels the heart to be, according to the necessities of time and place, now affable and courteous, not sharp and stinging, with a proper measure in gentleness or reproof, as need may be…" – *St. Angela Merici (Bernard O'Reilly. St. Angela Merici, and the Ursulines (1880) Pollard & Moss)*

As we strive to live a holy life, a virtuous life, we may be concerned about how to interact with those who lead a seemingly very different life. Perhaps it's scary to be around neighbors or family members who don't believe what we do…we don't know how to talk with them in a meaningful way without seeming as if we are "holier-than-thou" or judgmental. We feel uneasy and uncomfortable because it takes more energy to be around people that don't fill our cup. It's easy to say we hate the sin but love the sinner—but how do we put that into practice? It will typically look like making it clear, one time, that we don't agree with their choices or lifestyle but continuing to interact with them in a reasonable manner. Of course, we can't lead children into scandal, so it depends on our state in life. But the best thing is to pray and discern how God wants us to live out virtue as a witness to the Truth and freedom found in Christ, which includes loving sacrifice.

Everyone has dignity as a human person, and encountering them, as Christ did, will help us to live a more virtuously affable life. We keep our senses searching for the "divine appointments" that God places before us. Divine appointments are those seemingly chance meetings with a long-lost friend, weird coincidences where we keep seeing the same person over and over again, or a perfectly lined-up situation to speak with someone.

In His Goodness, God will never *not* give us an opportunity to magnify Him that He wanted us to take. When we come upon those opportunities, we must choose affability and gentleness so that a deep friendship may be built as trust in each other grows. We can model compassion so that others are able to trust in God's mercy. Often times, many people that claim not to believe in God really have a trust issue. We can't help others come to know Christ if we don't trust Him too, so we strive to believe that He will work things out for Good, even if we can't see it. We share our brokenness and the ways that Jesus has transformed our wounds so that others can believe it can happen for them too! Perhaps our growth in affability can be rooted in our ability to be vulnerable and open with the ways God has loved us—and continues to love us!

Read Ephesians 4 – what kind of friend are you? Do you try to keep your eyes and heart open for people needing a true, meaningful friend? Reach out to someone today and plan an in person meet-up. Focus on becoming friends—you don't have to solve any problems; trust that God has that under control.

AFFABILITY: DAY 14

Praying a daily Rosary is part of Magnify, because if we seek to magnify the Lord, Mary is the best example for us. The second joyful mystery of the Rosary is The Visitation, and the fruit of meditating on it is "love of neighbor."

In those days Mary set out and went with haste to a Judean town in the hill country, where she entered the house of Zechariah and greeted Elizabeth. When Elizabeth heard Mary's greeting, the child leaped in her womb. And Elizabeth was filled with the Holy Spirit and exclaimed with a loud cry, "Blessed are you among women, and blessed is the fruit of your womb. And why has this happened to me, that the mother of my Lord comes to me? For as soon as I heard the sound of your greeting, the child in my womb leaped for joy. And blessed is she who believed that there would be a fulfillment of what was spoken to her by the Lord." – *Luke 1:39-45*

CCC 1397 The Eucharist commits us to the poor. To receive in truth the Body and Blood of Christ given up for us, we must recognize Christ in the poorest, his brethren: You have tasted the Blood of the Lord, yet you do not recognize your brother, . . . You dishonor this table when you do not judge worthy of sharing your food someone judged worthy to take part in this meal. . . . God freed you from all your sins and invited you here, but you have not become more merciful. *(St. John Chrysostom)*

Mary, unexpectedly pregnant, didn't dwell on her own burdens and uncertain future. She went to visit Elizabeth. Through her feminine genius of receptivity, sensitivity, generosity, and maternity, Mary knew that bringing the Lord to Elizabeth was the best way to share joy. Mary spent time with Elizabeth, cared for her in pregnancy, and glorified God in praise and thanksgiving. Both women kept each other company in the waiting. The waiting for Jesus, the waiting for labor and birth…the waiting for Heaven. The word company comes from Latin, meaning "together-bread."Through the example of Jesus, Mary, and the early church, we are called to be in the company of our neighbor: to break bread together.

Nowhere is this more prominently lived out than at Mass. While life does require patience for the final Beatific Vision, we know that in sharing the True Bread, we are able to have a brief foretaste of eternal joy! We should keep in mind that being at Mass is the closest we get to Heaven here, because angels and saints are there praising God with us! As part of our pursuit of affability, sharing with others about our own experience with Jesus in the Eucharist is important.

We are called to forgo our desires to wallow in our difficulties, even if we feel isolated. It's often in the moments we are inward focused that someone else needs our love and attention. We can tell who that person may be when we are free to pick up on the subtle nudges God gives us in prayer through our humble openness to His Will. Let us seek to follow the Blessed Mother's example, magnifying the Lord through our life and seeking His life in others. When we are hospitable, we welcome guests, of which the greatest is Christ in our neighbor. As we pray the Rosary mystery of the Visitation, we could try to mediate on the ways we can practice affability more naturally in our lives.

Consider

Have you had instances where you needed to focus less on the challenges you were facing, and instead focus on those around you? How did you welcome them? What can you find in celebrating the joys of others? What parts of your natural personality help and hinder your affability? Encourage others to come back to Mass and remind them to pray with the Saints —most of our participation at Mass happens internally.

WEEKLY REFLECTIONS

Gratitude

St. Josephine Bakhita

WEEK 3-GRATITUDE
St. Josephine Bakhita

Mortifications	S	M	T	W	T	F	S
DAILY PRAYER (30 MIN) MAGNIFICAT, LITANY, ROSARY	✝	✝	✝	✝	✝	✝	✝
DAILY MASS							
CONFESSION (MONTHLY)							
ADORATION (WEEKLY)							
NO MAKEUP			✝		✝		
MEATLESS FASTING					✝		
INTENTIONAL WALK WITH FRIEND OR HUSBAND							
CONNECT WITH PERSON WHO CAME TO MIND IN PRAYER							
OTHER:							
OTHER:							
OTHER:							

Other Daily Mortifications to Remember

- ONLY CHRISTIAN/CLASSICAL MUSIC AND PODCASTS
- ONLY RELIGIOUS PROGRAMMING IN MODERATION
- NO WEIGHING ON A SCALE
- NO SWEETS, ALCOHOL, OR SNACKS IN BETWEEN MEALS
- NO SOCIAL MEDIA
- NO UNNECESSARY SHOPPING
- _____
- _____
-

I am offering my intentions for:

S ● _____
M ● _____
T ● _____
W ● _____
T ● _____
F ● _____
S ● _____
Other ● _____

Express

Use this space to journal, draw, or otherwise express your thoughts on this week's virtue. Spend some time listening to the Holy Spirit, perhaps in Adoration, and capture whatever He brings to mind or lays on your heart.

GRATITUDE: DAY 15

This week our topic is gratitude. As we let go of the desire for more, we find joy and peace. Gratitude is necessary to magnify the Lord.

All your works give you thanks, LORD and your faithful bless you. They speak of the glory of your reign and tell of your mighty works, making known to the sons of men your mighty acts, the majestic glory of your rule. Your reign is a reign for all ages, your dominion for all generations. The LORD is trustworthy in all his words, and loving in all his works. The LORD supports all who are falling and raises up all who are bowed down. – *Psalm 145:10-14*

Recall the part of the Mass when the priest says, "Let us give thanks to the Lord Our God." Then, we the people respond, "It is right and just!" Giving thanks to the Lord, the priest continues, is our duty and our salvation. Our hope for salvation has in it a life of gratitude lived for God because of the sacrifice on the cross that Christ made to rejoin the human race with God. Without that sacrifice, we had an unpayable debt to God. We, as a people, chose knowledge over trust in God. Ever since the fall from grace in the Garden of Eden, humans have been disconnected and in a continual struggle to find re-communion with God. That is original sin, the ingrained disconnection from God's perfect will.

Jesus Christ's incarnation made Holy Communion possible—both in the eternal sense and in the physical sense. The Eucharist is our remembrance of Christ's sacrifice and our thanksgiving to God for life and the ability to have a relationship with Him. The word "Eucharist" comes from the Greek word for "grace" (kharis/charis) and the prefix "eu," which means "well." Although the translation of well there means "good", in English it doubles as a point to consider of how we are to draw Living Water from the well of Jesus' mercy. He pours His mercy into our souls most especially when we receive His True Presence. Each time we participate in Mass, we recall the truth that God is the source of all good and it is our duty to show Him gratitude.

The Lord reaches down, extending mercy, to the human race through the Sacraments, especially at the Mass where Heaven and Earth meet. We meet His embrace with willing minds and receptive souls, even when life suffering is great. Even if the Lord doesn't seem to answer prayers as we want Him to, He will never not give us something we truly need. We can be grateful for this.

Consider

How have you experienced spiritual and physical strengthening through receiving the Blessed Sacrament? How does your life's priorities reflect gratitude for all the Lord's goodness? Do you seem to still be waiting for God's provision? Include "Remembrance" by Matt Maher as a part of your prayer today if you'd like.

GRATITUDE: DAY 16

Adoration is gratitude for love, gratitude for everything that gives us life and hope of eternity. Gratitude leads us to worship God for all that He is.

CCC 2096: Adoration is the first act of the virtue of religion. To adore God is to acknowledge him as God, as the Creator and Savior, the Lord and Master of everything that exists, as infinite and merciful Love. "You shall worship the Lord your God, and him only shall you serve," says Jesus, citing Deuteronomy (6:13). (Luke 4:8)

2097: To adore God is to acknowledge, in respect and absolute submission, the "nothingness of the creature" who would not exist but for God. To adore God is to praise and exalt him and to humble oneself, as Mary did in the Magnificat, confessing with gratitude that he has done great things and holy is his name (Luke 1:46-49). The worship of the one God sets man free from turning in on himself, from the slavery of sin and the idolatry of the world.

A major piece of Magnify 90 is humbly giving up worldly things, to detach from it while simultaneously attaching ourselves to God. We choose God freely. Why would we do this, if not because we recognize Him as Creator and source of all good? The word "worship," in part, comes from the word "worth," meaning "to turn into, turn back to." Such as, "that computer is worth $500," meaning it could be sold and turned into $500 to use to buy a side of beef for a family to eat over several months. In the example, we sacrifice the computer to get the $500 to buy the meat. Sacrifice is at the heart of worship, because we give something up to get something else.

The worship of God is to recognize He is worth something to us. So what is God worth? As the creator of everything, He is worth everything. In a sense, we must give everything up to be with Everything. How do we do that? We must acknowledge we are unable to do so on our own because we are only a part of creation, not in control of everything. Yet, we are given dominion over creation as humans made in God's own image. The answer to this mystery is gratitude as the sacrifice. Recognizing we are only stewards, not owners, of everything given to us allows us to be able to care for the created world, while at the same time knowing we owe it all to God.

We cannot "turn in on ourselves." To worship God, we must look outward. We make small offerings here or there to help others, to share what we have, to offer prayers, and to seek unity. Our mortifications help us to focus on what will help us become the saints God calls us to be—trusting in God and gratitude for His provision and grace. We have life, we have nourishment, we have human relationship. We have our faith! We are chosen and called to be a light for the world that does not fully know Him. When we feel spiritually weak, we must ask Him to give us the graces necessary to carry on with the mission entrusted to us. And when we feel spiritually strong, we must be thankful and recognize the Lord as the source of this strength!

If we have lived a way of life for so long and then suddenly make a change, that may give others pause. They may ask us, "What made you change that?!" To which we can say something like, "The love of God! I want to simplify me and magnify Him!" When our lives start to look differently because of virtue, which alone is a witness to God's Truth, Goodness, and Beauty.

While it is certainly hard to be a Christian in today's age full of distraction and relativism, we know that whatever trial may come our way in this life holds nothing to the glorious everlasting life to come. When we feel the Way and Truth and Life is too hard, those are the moments to draw closer to God, thanking Him for the opportunity to connect our suffering to Christ's cross. Let the example of Mary, Our Mother, and the communion of sinners turned Saints be our encouragement.

Reflect on the comfort you find in food or drink. Recognize that so many in the world eat, on a daily basis, things you'd never want to eat, period, and drink muddy or contaminated water. Each time you're tempted to give up on one of your mortifications, think of Christ thirsting for you. Have you ever recognized physical hunger as a stand-in for true hunger for Christ? That feeling in the pit of your stomach invites you to turn to the Lord as the Bread of Life, knowing human food will ultimately leave you needing still more.

GRATITUDE: DAY 17

Reflect on the life of St. Josephine Bakhita, who was scarred 114 times by slave owners "branding" her with razor blades and rubbing salt in the wounds. She is a feminine genius of gratitude.

"If I were to meet the slave traders who kidnapped me and even those who tortured me...I would kneel and kiss their hands, for if that did not happen, I would not be a Christian and religious today. The Lord has loved me so much. We must love everyone." – *St. Josephine Margaret Bakhita*

Bakhita was in captivity so long and tortured so much that she forgot her own name. Bakhita is Arabic for "fortunate"; at first it was ironic when given to her by captors, but she later would say it described her accurately. After going to Italy with a girl to whom she was enslaved, Bakhita met Catholic nuns. Bakhita came to know the Lord, gained freedom, and received the sacraments. She joined the Canossian religious order and blessed the lives of so many people through humble service. Her ultimate story is one of forgiveness and gratitude, joy and love.

This is like what Christ calls us to in the life of the Church—seeking forgiveness for our sins, being grateful for mercy, and living a life of virtue. We also extend forgiveness to others so that we can be truly free. Josephine, her baptismal name, never could have experienced true freedom if she had clung to anger or resentment toward the slave traders or "owners". Through looking at everything that happens as an ability to grow closer to God and more Christ-like, we find true freedom when we are open to love, grateful for life, and able to experience peace only brought by Him.

While it is hard to say and hard to hear, the phrase "everything happens for a reason," is apt. St. Josephine shows us that God can use even the sins of others to bring good in the fallen world. It's important to note that He never wills evil but permits it to exist because sin must have the ability to exist or else love couldn't. Love is found in freedom because we have the ability to deny it. When others deny love, and deny God, of course we are affected. Yet, the Lord calls us to Himself through all situations. We can only control our reaction when others hurt us, or even when someone we love dies. It is our virtuous choice to be grateful for the existence of love amidst situations that the world might say gives us a "right" to be spiteful or despairing.

Walls built from resentment block out joy. We must forgive others, as we are forgiven; not hold grudges. When the cause of our sadness is no obvious fault of a human—extreme as death from disease or accident, or as minor as a rain storm on the day of a picnic—we trust that God wants good for us all, always. It's just our limited understanding of what good means. In our limited understanding of God's omnipresence and omnipotence, we must trust that both what's good for us and what we consider to be suffering can be the same thing.

We will certainly be sad, even distraught for a time. Our love and longing for those who've gone before us must still point us to hope in eternity; it is what we're made for. Gratitude for life as a gift will keep us upright in the storms of life. We root our joy in God alone—we can find it in others, but its starting point must always be God. It's very hard to live that out, but through our virtues we can joyfully magnify the Lord even in times of sorrow. Our lives will be much happier when we accept all things in our path as an opportunity to love God and love others. In fact, some of the best opportunities to magnify the Lord are found in living gratitude through things the world says should turn us away from Him.

What grudges are you harboring, even if only a little, toward humans or God? Can you identify areas where selfishness or entitlement have a grip on your life? How does that affect virtue? How can you be joyful in your life today, despite the scars?

GRATITUDE: DAY 18

he Christian faith spreads by the grace of the Holy Spirit and the virtue of believers that inspires others. The Catechism paragraphs 75-95 are extremely helpful on this topic.

So, as you received Christ Jesus the Lord, walk in him, rooted in him and built upon him and established in the faith as you were taught, abounding in thanksgiving. See to it that no one captivate you with an empty, seductive philosophy according to human tradition, according to the elemental powers of the world and not according to Christ. – *Colossians 2:6-8*

CCC 78: This living transmission, accomplished in the Holy Spirit, is called Tradition, since it is distinct from Sacred Scripture, though closely connected to it. Through Tradition, "the Church, in her doctrine, life and worship, perpetuates and transmits to every generation all that she herself is, all that she believes." (DV 8 § 1) "The sayings of the holy Fathers are a witness to the life-giving presence of this Tradition, showing how its riches are poured out in the practice and life of the Church, in her belief and her prayer." (DV 8 § 3)

We have to strive for the Christian mentality back toward changing the world, rather than the world changing us. We are too frequently seduced by the technologies we invent, the power we claim as our own, and the comfort we create. But when we follow Sacred Tradition and read Sacred Scripture, we can love rather than simply tolerate. It takes virtue to truly love, while tolerating is for those simply with values. Christian virtues direct our actions toward Truth and the end for which we were created, and values are just an appreciation for something good without having to get involved. If we just value something or someone, we let the world change us as values change. To strive as co-creators with God, to "change the fallen world", we need to pursue virtue, which never changes and always involves our grateful participation.

"Liturgical Living" is one way to follow Sacred Tradition and will help us emulate the life habits of so many Saints. We can avoid just appreciating Christianity and instead actually live it out. Rather than ordering our days around what we want to get done, we order our days around the sacraments, the daily Mass readings and liturgy of the hours, the feast days, the fasts and ember days, the solemn observances, and liturgical seasons—all handed down through the generations as a way to develop discipline toward holiness that manifests itself as virtue. They are not simply things to be done with a perfectionist attitude. They are ways to walk in Christ's life, hoping in Him, and being grateful for His mercy.

Feminine geniuses crave companionship, friendship, and intimacy (physical, emotional, or spiritual). Through these relationships we can magnify the Lord like Mary did. We can bring Jesus to others through our way of life. Sadly, though, the enemy tries to seduce us away from God's good intention for relationship, and into a disordered attachment to others' opinions or values which change with the times. Even if we try hard not to let others' worldly opinions influence our behavior, the reality is that spiritual attacks often come in the form of convincing us we aren't good enough, we don't have enough, or we aren't loved. Perhaps we even start to wonder if we are crazy for standing up for ancient Truths that others tell us are outdated.

Sisters, these are lies. God has made us good, we have enough in Him, and we are loved beyond measure! Do not be seduced by human tradition, but cling to Sacred Tradition; abound in thanksgiving!

Has lukewarmness ever settled into your soul? How have you accepted it with complacency? How do you try to flee from it? When you analyze your life, do you notice virtue increasing? What liturgical practices can you adopt in your home? How aware are you of the celebration of the saints' lives within the church calendar? Investigate ways to live that can increase your ability to practice gratitude for Tradition.

GRATITUDE: DAY 19

Prayerfulness as a virtue will be a topic later, but for now, we can meditate upon the connection between prayer and gratitude. Because we are still on earth, prayer is our best way to communicate our gratefulness to God.

CCC 2098: The acts of faith, hope, and charity enjoined by the first commandment are accomplished in prayer. Lifting up the mind toward God is an expression of our adoration of God: prayer of praise and thanksgiving, intercession and petition. Prayer is an indispensable condition for being able to obey God's commandments. "[We] ought always to pray and not lose heart." *(Luke 18:1)*

"Seeing the sun, the moon and the stars, I said to myself: who could be the Master of these beautiful things? And I felt a great desire to see him, to know him and to pay him homage…" – *St. Josephine Bakhita*

What is our intention when we pray? Do we seek answers; do we ask for certain desires? Neither is necessarily bad, because Jesus does tell us to seek, knock, and ask (Matthew 7)—but the purpose of prayer is relationship with God. Our prayer should express our desire to be with God, just for the sake of being with Him. Gratitude is a prayer, and prayer should be gratitude. It's actually the highest form of prayer because it allows us to rest, mostly in a non-tangible way, upon Christ's chest like the Beloved Disciple did at the Last Supper. We simply find ourselves contemplating the Goodness of God and dwelling in gratitude for His all-loving desires for us.

God created us and we have an intrinsic desire to be with Him who has our very existence as His interest. The closer we draw near to Him, the more we want to follow His will because we recognize He loves us. This doesn't make mortification easier—often it may get harder in some areas as God refines us and the enemy works harder to tempt us—but it makes us more willing to desire the fruit that can come from it. When we leave space in our physical, emotional, and spiritual lives for God, we leave more room for gratitude and joy. Our virtues help us align our will to God's will. Gratitude keeps us hopeful, which strengthens our trusting relationship with our Heavenly Father.

Consider

How is your prayer commitment going? What are you lazy or procrastinating in? Can you be more intentional in the ways you connect with the Lord? Start a gratitude journal. How can you contemplate God? How do you sense Him? What can you offer Him today? Close your eyes and imagine laying your head on His chest, His Most Sacred Heart.

GRATITUDE: DAY 20

Avoiding disordered consumption of unnecessary knowledge and media helps us stay calmer and more grateful. Curiosity is a vice when we fall into the sin of prideful thinking. If we aren't even in a position to properly and charitably correct others, it's not virtuous to sit around discussing their faults.

"Be good, love the Lord, pray for those who do not know Him. What a great grace it is to know God!" – *St. Josephine Bakhita*

Therefore let us be grateful for receiving a kingdom that cannot be shaken, and thus let us offer to God acceptable worship, with reverence and awe. – *Hebrews 12:28*

One may watch other people's actions or inquire into them, with a good intent, either for one's own good—that is in order to be encouraged to better deeds by the deeds of our neighbor—or for our neighbor's good—that is in order to correct him, if he do anything wrong, according to the rule of charity and the duty of one's position. This is praiseworthy, according to Hebrews 10:24, "Consider one another to provoke unto charity and to good works." But to observe our neighbor's faults with the intention of looking down upon them, or of detracting them, or even with no further purpose than that of disturbing them, is sinful: hence it is written (Proverbs 24:15), "Lie not in wait, nor seek after wickedness in the house of the just, nor spoil his rest." – *St. Thomas Aquinas, Summa Theologiae II-II Q167, a2, r3*

In today's age of constant media, it's easy to get bogged down with the problems—even those within the Church. We worry that the world is senseless, that people are messing everything up, or that it's all spiraling out of control. Because we actually have very little control over other people, we fear that their unfaithfulness, or perceived lack of holiness, will encroach upon our path—which is hard enough without obstacles from others. This is what Satan wants. He desires chaos and worry. Rather than let the devil continue to distract us, we must focus on our own personal holiness and not let the woes of the world divert us from the gratitude God invites us to have for our life, our faith, and our love.

We know that Jesus Christ has already overcome death, and the devil won't prevail over the gates of Heaven. This means we should avoid negativity, instead looking for the good in even the people we don't think are doing the right thing. Speaking the truth and admonishing the sinner are very necessary, but can we more effectively invite others into a life of virtue through our peace and unshakeable joy? This will be more successful, because truth is easier to swallow when it's enveloped in love. We shouldn't spend our precious time and mental space on issues we can't do anything about. When they do naturally come to our attention, prayer and fasting are the route we should take, rather than judgmental gossip.

We should strive to simply cooperate with the graces of the sacraments instituted by Christ, which are our ladder to salvation. The promise of Heaven is there for us all; no one can take that away from us. We are the ones who chose to accept or deny the mercy offered. Even if the priesthood seemingly falls apart, and sacraments aren't offered in the ordinary way,

God will always give us everything we need! It's beyond our understanding, but His mercy and grace are outside what we can see. This is what we must be grateful for! Every song we sing, every action we take, every step we walk—these should glorify God! When we recognize our worldly idolatry, when we see our sin, we crawl back to the Lord, asking for forgiveness, and then we walk upright in gratitude for His mercy. Living this type of life, magnifying the Lord in this way, will change the world.

What does living your life for the greater glory of God mean to you? Are you letting anything into your mental space that distracts but serves no real purpose? What thing can you be thankful for today, even though the world would say it's negative / hard / sad / uncomfortable?

GRATITUDE: DAY 21

Our ability to offer God a sacrifice of praise and mercy is found in being grateful for His mercy. To cling to Him, rather than treat created goods as gods, is how we make a true sacrifice.

CCC 2099: It is right to offer sacrifice to God as a sign of adoration and gratitude, supplication and communion: "Every action done so as to cling to God in communion of holiness, and thus achieve blessedness, is a true sacrifice. (St. Augustine)"

2100: Outward sacrifice, to be genuine, must be the expression of spiritual sacrifice: "The sacrifice acceptable to God is a broken spirit..." (Psalm 51:17) The prophets of the Old Covenant often denounced sacrifices that were not from the heart or not coupled with love of neighbor. (Amos 5/Isaiah 1) Jesus recalls the words of the prophet Hosea: "I desire mercy, and not sacrifice." (Hosea 6:6) The only perfect sacrifice is the one that Christ offered on the cross as a total offering to the Father's love and for our salvation. (Hebrews 9:13-14) By uniting ourselves with his sacrifice we can make our lives a sacrifice to God.

To accept the salvation offered to us by Christ's redeeming work on the cross we have to be humble enough to even recognize that only God is God. We must thank Him through sacrifices offered in gratitude. We are not called to the ministerial priesthood as women, but we are baptized with the calling of priest, prophet, and king. We fulfill our role as priest, following the example of Christ and Mary, when we offer sacrifices in our daily lives. From the above passage, we can tell that God wants a sacrifice of mercy, praise, and humility more than burnt offerings or other tangible things. The merciful sacrifice God asks of us is found in our virtue, in the way we magnify Him, in the way we habitually choose to do good joyfully despite physical or mental hardships. How do we show selfless love to others?

Men are called to offer sacrifice in their own unique ways (especially those men that are priests at the altar), and women, ours, as is our complementary nature. The work we do in practicing virtue is tangibly seen through our genius of maternity. Whether spiritual or physical, we are mothers nurturing His life in others. Being sensitive to the needs of those around us, we can tell when people need a break from the harshness of others. We must stop demanding what we want when we want it and adhering to our own rigid ideas of how things should go: how long an appointment should take, how fast a secretary should move, or how fast a learning child should solve a math homework problem. We must be grateful for those right in front of us, because God deemed it worthy that they be in our sphere of influence at that moment.

How blessed are we to get to let the light of Christ shine out of us into the world as tabernacles of the Holy Spirit?

When we could lash out or severely punish, when we could slam a door or leave abruptly, God asks us to show mercy. Mercy is more than justice; it's beyond what's fair. How does He show us mercy when we deserve a "door slam" or walking away for our sins?

Consider

Are you still clinging to some worldly attachment? How do you cling to God in "communion of holiness"? Are you grateful for the sacrament of confession? Read through chapters 4 and 5 of Lumen Gentium for more of the Church's teaching about the offerings of lay people and the way we are called to holiness – it can be found on the Vatican's website.

WEEKLY REFLECTIONS

Magnanimity

St. Teresa of Calcutta

WEEK 4-MAGNANIMITY
St. Teresa of Calcutta

Mortifications	S	M	T	W	T	F	S
DAILY PRAYER (30 MIN) MAGNIFICAT, LITANY, ROSARY	✝	✝	✝	✝	✝	✝	✝
DAILY MASS							
CONFESSION (MONTHLY)							
ADORATION (WEEKLY)							
NO MAKEUP		✝			✝		
MEATLESS FASTING						✝	
INTENTIONAL WALK WITH FRIEND OR HUSBAND							
CONNECT WITH PERSON WHO CAME TO MIND IN PRAYER							
OTHER:							
OTHER:							
OTHER:							

Other Daily Mortifications to Remember

- ONLY CHRISTIAN/CLASSICAL MUSIC AND PODCASTS
- ONLY RELIGIOUS PROGRAMMING IN MODERATION
- NO WEIGHING ON A SCALE
- NO SWEETS, ALCOHOL, OR SNACKS IN BETWEEN MEALS
- NO SOCIAL MEDIA
- NO UNNECESSARY SHOPPING
- _____
- _____
- _____

I am offering my intentions for:

S ● _____
M ● _____
T ● _____
W ● _____
T ● _____
F ● _____
S ● _____
Other ● _____

Express Use this space to journal, draw, or otherwise express your thoughts on this week's virtue. Spend some time listening to the Holy Spirit, perhaps in Adoration, and capture whatever He brings to mind or lays on your heart.

MAGNANIMITY: DAY 22

As we enter into the week with magnanimity as our theme, let us start with the Catholic Dictionary (Fr. P. Stravinskas, OSV 2002) definition to help us grasp the meaning of this virtue.
Magnanimity: The virtue enabling one to perform outstanding, morally good actions not for recognition but for love of God and neighbor. Prudence directs magnanimity, which supports the cardinal virtue of fortitude. Only those who perform the other virtues regularly are usually able to be magnanimous.

CCC 1804: Human virtues are firm attitudes, stable dispositions, habitual perfections of intellect and will that govern our actions, order our passions, and guide our conduct according to reason and faith. They make possible ease, self-mastery, and joy in leading a morally good life. The virtuous man is he who freely practices the good. The moral virtues are acquired by human effort. They are the fruit and seed of morally good acts; they dispose all the powers of the human being for communion with divine love.

Virtues are habits of doing good, but the more we practice them, the more our whole life is affected. It becomes easier to do good joyfully, even when life is hard or stressful. We must make conscious efforts to do good things and live out moral truths. When we do that, we can grow closer to God. As He is the source of all good, we need God to even be able to know what is good. The virtues that enable us to grow closer to God are faith, hope, and charity (love). Those theological virtues fill us through prayer and grace—which of course includes the sacraments. This is why it's so important to have a daily prayer life and frequent confession and Eucharist when striving for a virtuous life.

The virtue of magnanimity calls for hearts purified in intention and actions done with selfless love and joy. To be magnanimous is to have a "large soul." A magnanimous woman seeks to do the will of God—regardless of the glory or shame it brings by the world's standards—knowing God's will is the only way to holiness. Magnanimity gives us the ability to practice our faith despite the culture around us that continues to grow in relativism and seemingly devalues faith.

A budding seed, or perhaps blooming flower, of magnanimity in our soul brought us to reading this book. Magnanimity creates in the soul the desire to magnify the Lord. We don't want to be lukewarm; we don't strive for just "good enough;" we are women seeking the full glory of God.

Yet how often we vacillate between feeling inadequate and unqualified to feeling like we must do all the things and help all the people. Neither is true! A truly magnanimous woman knows the source of all good, and only out of love for God does she strive to confidently use all the gifts she's been given—not less and not more. Take heart, sister, doing great things often doesn't mean big things.

Worldly achievements, temporal approval, and human honor are not the goals we chase after, but if God wills us to have those things, the heroic use of them is to bring others to His love through them as well. Our good deeds are only for God's glory. Truly, our "greatness" is based on the commandment to love God with our whole being and to love our neighbor as ourselves.

Consider

What kind of effort have you exerted in the past toward acquiring human virtues? Do you have more habits that help you or hurt you along the path of sainthood? What kind of effort are you putting in these 90 days? As you detach from worldly things, do you feel the freedom to receive Divine Love more openly?

MAGNANIMITY: DAY 23

The life of Mother Teresa is a modern example of a magnanimous soul. She was both humble and bold. She did the heroic to bring God glory, not herself.

"God didn't call me to be successful. God called me to be faithful." – *St. Teresa of Calcutta (Leo Maasburg. Teresa of Calcutta: A Personal Portrait (2015) Ignatius)*

"Make us realize that it is only by frequent deaths of ourselves and our self-centered desires that we can come to live more fully; for it is only by dying with you that we can rise with you." – *St. Teresa of Calcutta (Jean Maalouf, editor. Mother Teresa: Essential Writings (2001) Orbis)*

"We are at His disposal. If He wants you to be sick in bed, if He wants you to proclaim His word in the street, if He wants you to clean the toilets all day, that's all right, everything is all right. We must say, "I belong to you. You can do whatever you like." This is our strength and this is the joy of the Lord." – *St. Teresa of Calcutta (Jean Maalouf, editor. Mother Teresa: Essential Writings (2001) Orbis)*

Magnanimity is living a life full of virtue, amidst the challenges, in hopes that we encounter Christ more fully. It calls on us to practice fortitude as well because of those challenges. Fortitude is the strength to do good in the face of evil, and it requires commitment to God's will in the midst of difficulty. In an extreme case, it would give us the heroic virtue necessary to be a martyr. Because most of us reading this are likely not called to martyrdom, magnanimity is our living out a smaller, daily martyrdom. Dying to self for the freedom to proclaim, by our simple living, that God is all Good and deserving of all our love and devotion. In our current practice of self-denial / mortification we are trying to overcome the attachments that keep us self-centered. We're leaning into God's grace so that we become more and more selfless, like St. Teresa of Calcutta, who sought to magnify the Lord in her work with the poor, sick, and marginalized of India.

What might our "big soul" look like when it's lived simply? It's the small, yet virtuous choices made each day. We wake up when our alarm goes off. We ask how another is doing, rather than complaining about our day. We keep trivial grievances to ourselves when it's more uplifting to show mercy. We pack lunches when kids forget, yet again, joyfully. We go to daily Mass even when it seems inconvenient. We check on a neighbor who lives alone. We do the dishes at the house in which we are a guest. We change 15 diapers with a loving smile. We stop petty gossip in its tracks. We invite others to sit with us. We help an elderly person with her grocery cart at the store. We help pass out food to the poor and strike up a conversation in recognition of their dignity. We correct a child mercifully and firmly, rather than with wrath. We use the short time we have with strangers in passing to brighten their day in any number of small ways. Being made for greatness doesn't mean doing news-worthy "charity," it means taking what God has given us and using it for what He intended (though it may sometimes make headlines).

Over the past weeks, we've been praying as Mary did, acknowledging each of us are *ancilla domini* – the handmaid of the Lord. When we are in relationship with God through prayer and the sacraments, we can listen for the ways He wants to use us. Then magnanimity motivates us to boldly do that, despite any hardships it may cause us, because it is for Him. We may "lose" money, power, prestige, and even, unfortunately, relationships at times. God never promised us ease in our earthly life, but if it's His will, it's worth it. Heaven is our goal, and this causes us to live a certain way.

Do you see your whole life as a way to bring God glory? What gifts and time do you have that aren't being directed to a saintly end? What distractions in your life are keeping you from living magnanimously? Decide to do a little something with a big soul today.

MAGNANIMITY: DAY 24

To practice virtue is a choice. It is an assent to the Truth. We must continue to climb the mountain of virtue, never settling or thinking we've arrived. We keep chipping away at the rough edges of our souls, together with God, so that all that remains at the end of our life is the best self we can offer our Creator.

CCC 1803: "Whatever is true, whatever is honorable, whatever is just, whatever is pure, whatever is lovely, whatever is gracious, if there is any excellence, if there is anything worthy of praise, think about these things." (Phil 4:8) A virtue is an habitual and firm disposition to do the good. It allows the person not only to perform good acts, but to give the best of himself. The virtuous person tends toward the good with all his sensory and spiritual powers; he pursues the good and chooses it in concrete actions. "The goal of a virtuous life is to become like God." (St. Gregory of Nyssa)

The desire to think of the true, honorable, just, pure, lovely, gracious, and excellent comes from God. With so many attachments stripped away during these 90 days, there are silent moments to sense the encouragement the Holy Spirit breathes into our souls. We should also be making time for more sacraments, where we really encounter Christ and receive actual grace. What we were doing spiritually before Magnify 90 should not be what we are doing now. Whether we were solidly devout or still figuring out our level of buy-in on the whole Catholic thing, the effort we are putting into our relationship with God should still be increasing. We all still have work to do, taking small steps to enlarge our souls.

Read a new spiritual book or a psalm a day. Take up praying part (or all) of the Divine Office. Listen to a homily online. Sign up for another Holy Hour. Read about a new-to-you saint. Go to Mass another day of the week. Call instead of texting to say hi to a family member. Send a letter of gratitude to a religious. Make time and space for stillness. Small things are heroic too when we do them for the glory of God. These will help us to overcome ourselves, and we will end up being more joyful in the face of tedious chores, hard sufferings, and exhausting work. Virtues take practice and greatness of soul takes the greatest practice. If the goal we have for ourselves is heaven, our lives on earth must look like it!

When adding spiritual practices we must recognize the balance needed in our humanity, and a good spiritual mentor or direction can help with this discernment. The struggle opposed to magnanimity can go to two extremes. We can suffer from a kind of "reverse-pride" that is disguised as (false) humility and ends up being pusillanimous. This is having a "small-soul"—being too afraid to trust God's grace. We end up being tepid and indifferent to the ways we should be bringing God glory. Perhaps we don't think our little lives in our little towns matter. We may feel anxious about speaking the truth about God or create reasons we are too busy to help with a ministry, when actual fear is driving the decision. We may feel too self-conscious to wear a small religious item at work, avoid meat on Friday at a catered-in office lunch, or ask others to pray with us before a restaurant meal. But if we feel a call to do these things, let magnanimity prevail; even though little, they are great!

The opposite side of the spectrum could find us trying to embrace all the good things with the mentality that we should and must do it all, viewing our humanity as limitless. We could appear magnanimous, but actually be suffering from vanity and pride. We could sign up to bake 300 mini-quiches for the shelter but end up working on them until 2 am and be prone to anger with our spouse the next day out of tiredness. We could end up leading yet another Marian study because we feel like we know a lot about Mary, yet it distracts us from our other commitment to the choir group.

Perhaps we invite girlfriends over for a weekly social women of faith night, even when it double books our family on nights of religious education class. Most often, vainglory is very sneaky. We think we are doing something good for God, but prudence has been neglected, and we end up in over our head when it may never have been His perfect will in the first place. Prudence must direct magnanimity.

Consider

How do you balance boldness with prudence? How can you participate more fully with how God is calling you to magnify Him? How can you continue to become who God has created you to be? If you want, add "Control" by For King & Country as part of your prayer today.

MAGNANIMITY: DAY 25

Let us continue our reflection on Mother Teresa's magnanimous spirituality as inspiration for our own.

"Never worry about numbers. Help one person at a time and always start with the person nearest you." – *St. Teresa of Calcutta (Chris Stewart & Tony Brandt. Casting Nets: Grow Your Faith by Sharing Your Faith (2015) Our Sunday Visitor)*

Mother Teresa is often cited as saying that 'to change the world you must go home and love your family.' What she really said at her acceptance speech for the Nobel Peace Prize was: "…we will begin to love. And we will love naturally, we will try to do something. First in our own home, next door neighbor in the country we live, in the whole world." *(Mother Teresa – Acceptance Speech. https://www.nobelprize.org/prizes/peace/1979/teresa/26200-mother-teresa-acceptance-speech-1979/)*

She also gave a lecture the next day, and said: "And so here I am talking with you – I want you to find the poor here, right in your own home first. And begin love there. Be that good news to your own people. And find out about your next-door neighbor – do you know who they are? …. Because I believe that love begins at home, and if we can create a home for the poor – I think that more and more love will spread. And we will be able through this understanding love to bring peace, be the good news to the poor. The poor in our own family first, in our country and in the world." *(Mother Teresa – Nobel Lecture. https://www.nobelprize.org/prizes/peace/1979/teresa/lecture/)*

St. Teresa means love should start at home, with people we are most naturally around, yet it doesn't end there. Our family are our brothers and sisters in Christ (see Matthew 12:46-50). Our family could effectively be the whole world, but it simply cannot be our mission to serve every one of the billions of people on earth. St. Teresa's point is that we don't have to leave the place we are to find those in need of Christ's love—though we should if prayer reveals a vocational call to foreign missions! The simplest way to bring light to the world is through encountering others in compassionate, selfless friendship— wherever God may be calling us to go.

Darkness will only be dispelled when we are connected to the light in others, so that single flames unite into giant fires upon the earth. When we all seek to do the small deeds with great love, God's grace abounds. An army of magnanimous Christians is needed to fight the enemy.

Having the feminine genius of sensitivity means we aren't closed off to the needs of others, but we don't have to help thousands of people. We just have to love the person in front of us right now, and the next day, and the day after that.

Do the next right thing. Love is willing the good of the other. The most perfect good is Heaven, so we truly must desire everyone to live eternity in God's presence.

Our magnanimous actions can help others to come to know Jesus Christ and the value they have as humans. The joy spread by our love must be so inviting that others learn that they too can cooperate in God's Goodness.

Consider

Have you prayed about your busyness and whether God is inviting you to spend some time being more available to others? Reflect on your in-person presence with your family and how screens factor in. Do your daily priorities align with the magnanimous soul you're cultivating? Do they flow through prayer turned into action?

If you'd like, include "Come Be My Light / Mother Teresa Song" by Liturgically Sound as part of your prayer today.

MAGNANIMITY: DAY 26

Mother Teresa wrote a prayer for Marian consecration that beautifully reminds us of the perfection of virtue in the Blessed Virgin Mary. When we seek to Magnify the Lord, her intercession is vital!

"Mary, I depend on you totally as a child on its mother, that in return you may possess me, protect me, and transform me into Jesus. May the light of your faith dispel the darkness of my mind; may your profound humility take the place of my pride; may your contemplation replace the distractions of my wandering imagination; and may your virtues take the place of my sins. Lead me deeper into the mystery of the cross that you may share your experience of Jesus's thirst with me.

O most pure heart of Mary, allow me to enter your heart, to share your interior life. You see and know my needs, help me to do "whatever Jesus tells me" ... that my human needs may be changed into thirst for God alone. I desire to discover, satiate, and proclaim Jesus's thirst, but I know all too well my weakness, nothingness, and sin. Mother, may this covenant of consecration with you be the hidden strength in my life that you may use me to satiate your Son to the full. Let this be my only joy... and you will be the cause of that joy." – *St. Teresa of Calcutta (Mother Teresa. Angelo D. Scolozzi, editor. Thirsting for God (2017) Servant)*

CCC 970: "Mary's function as mother of men in no way obscures or diminishes this unique mediation of Christ, but rather shows its power. But the Blessed Virgin's salutary influence on men . . . flows forth from the superabundance of the merits of Christ, rests on his mediation, depends entirely on it, and draws all its power from it." (Lumen Gentium 60) "No creature could ever be counted along with the Incarnate Word and Redeemer; but just as the priesthood of Christ is shared in various ways both by his ministers and the faithful, and as the one goodness of God is radiated in different ways among his creatures, so also the unique mediation of the Redeemer does not exclude but rather gives rise to a manifold cooperation which is but a sharing in this one source." (Lumen Gentium 62)

One of the things Catholics most often have to defend to others is our devotion to Mary. Non-Catholics may think we worship her or think she is equal to God. Perhaps some people struggle with the supernatural basis for Mary being our mother. Our prayer can be for those eyes to be opened to what Sacred Tradition and Sacred Scripture teach us about Mary. She is the new Ark of the Covenant, because it was the ark of the covenant that carried the Lord's presence on Earth, and her body carried Jesus Christ! Followers of Christ should hold Mary in high regard for many reasons, including that she is the queen of heaven written about in Revelation 12. She is called the Spouse of the Holy Spirit because it is through the union with the Holy Spirit that she conceived Jesus Christ. Christ is the King, and as His mother, she is our Queen Mother—pointing us to Him, bringing our intentions to Him. Thus, she is the Mother of the Church, the Body of Christ, and worthy of our devotion.

On the cross Jesus gave Mary, through John, to all apostles as their mother. Because of the relationship she has with her Divine Son and the Holy Spirit, she points us always to God. Loving Mary, asking for her prayers, meditating on her life, and trusting her to distribute our offerings of sacrifice is an appropriate relationship between children and their mother.

Mary is the moon, reflecting the light of the Son, never shining her own light. On our Magnify journey, we are trying to emulate Mary's Magnificat, letting our souls proclaim the greatness of God. If we are ever unsure of how to act in a situation, we can think, "How did Mary respond to God?" And to know how to answer this question we should be well-versed in her life. This is why the Rosary is such a beautiful prayer. By frequently meditating on the life of Jesus alongside Mary, we come to a deeper understanding of virtue and piety. She also asked us to pray it daily for the conversion of the world.

The Blessed Virgin Mary didn't ask to be the mother of the Word Incarnate; yet with her consent, the power of the Holy Spirit came upon her and the fullness of God filled her. So it is in our own lives; we must remove the obstacles that keep us from being able to say yes to the Holy Spirit. Using Mother Teresa's prayer of consecration to Mary, we too can ask Mary to take us under her protection, to make her perfection of virtue our own.

Have you prayed for the fullness of God to fill you? Where can you recognize that the power at work in you is God, and even more than you can imagine is possible? Look up some titles of Mary, such as through the Litany of Loreto, and find the one that speaks most to you. Ask for Mary's intercession under that title today. Consider reading CCC 963–975 for a more thorough teaching on Mary's relationship with the Church.

MAGNANIMITY: DAY 27

The parable of the talents is a great example of magnanimity versus pusillanimity.

[...] A man who was going on a journey called in his servants and entrusted his possessions to them. To one he gave five talents; to another, two; to a third, one—to each according to his ability. Then he went away. Immediately the one who received five talents went and traded with them, and made another five. Likewise, the one who received two made another two. But the man who received one went off and dug a hole in the ground and buried his master's money. After a long time the master of those servants came back and settled accounts with them. The one who had received five talents came forward bringing the additional five. He said, 'Master, you gave me five talents. See, I have made five more.' His master said to him, 'Well done, my good and faithful servant. Since you were faithful in small matters, I will give you great responsibilities. Come, share your master's joy.' [Then] the one who had received two talents also came forward and said, 'Master, you gave me two talents. See, I have made two more.' His master said to him, 'Well done, my good and faithful servant. Since you were faithful in small matters, I will give you great responsibilities. Come, share your master's joy.' Then the one who had received the one talent came forward and said, 'Master, I knew you were a demanding person, harvesting where you did not plant and gathering where you did not scatter; so out of fear I went off and buried your talent in the ground. Here it is back.' His master said to him in reply, 'You wicked, lazy servant! So you knew that I harvest where I did not plant and gather where I did not scatter? Should you not then have put my money in the bank so that I could have got it back with interest on my return? Now then! Take the talent from him and give it to the one with ten. For to everyone who has, more will be given and he will grow rich; but from the one who has not, even what he has will be taken away. And throw this useless servant into the darkness outside, where there will be wailing and grinding of teeth.' – *Matthew 25:14-30*

Think of a talent as a gift from God, especially the gift of love He has given us to share. God asks us to do something with that love. He doesn't want us to have the love—and subsequently the life, grace, and mercy—to keep to ourselves, hidden away from others. As we recognize the gifts we've been given, we must intentionally and responsibly cultivate them. This is practicing virtue. We no longer have any excuse for living a "small-souled" life; we can't claim ignorance. We're here learning more about the virtues that can help us answer the call to magnify the Lord, and care for the talents of our Lord as His stewards. Let us not settle into the mentality that good is good enough.

In order to "multiply" our talents, we have to invest time and energy. The last servant who buried his talent is small souled because he's too afraid or lazy, selfish or timid, to magnify what the master gave him. He doesn't act upon the fact that he is called for a purpose bigger than zero loss. Even if he's been trusted with only a small amount, that doesn't matter; it matters what he does with what he's been given. And in fact, the master in the parable was happy with the servants who did well with small matters. It brought him joy and he entrusted them with more responsibility. This is like us when we have been given a gift from the Holy Spirit and we let it feed our virtues. We put them into practice and multiply them. The Lord then trusts us with more and more, and we are able to be magnanimous.

We must persevere; even when we aren't seeing the fruits of our magnanimity, we must keep hoping! Hope is vital to magnanimity; hope that when the Lord returns, He will call us His good and faithful servants!

How does hope factor into your choices each day? What talents, blessings, and gifts from God have you "multiplied" and which are you letting go uncultivated? Have you lost hope that they'll grow? How did that happen and how can you be faithful in small matters?

MAGNANIMITY: DAY 28

When we promise God something, we should follow through. Of course, we won't be perfect in it, but that doesn't mean we shouldn't try. The continued getting up and trying again is the rhythm of life that makes a different in pursuing holiness.

CCC 2101: In many circumstances, the Christian is called to make promises to God. Baptism and Confirmation, Matrimony and Holy Orders always entail promises. Out of personal devotion, the Christian may also promise to God this action, that prayer, this alms-giving, that pilgrimage, and so forth. Fidelity to promises made to God is a sign of the respect owed to the divine majesty and of love for a faithful God.

Three times I begged the Lord about this, that it might leave me, but he said to me, "My grace is sufficient for you, for power is made perfect in weakness." I will rather boast most gladly of my weaknesses, in order that the power of Christ may dwell with me. Therefore, I am content with weaknesses, insults, hardships, persecutions, and constraints, for the sake of Christ; for when I am weak, then I am strong.
– 2 Corinthians 12:8-10

We're nearly a third of the way through our 90-day journey and yet the uphill battle against our attachments rages on. Perhaps we need to renew our promises to God and to ourselves. We set out in this desert to remind ourselves what our life is for: living like the Saints we are made to be: doing the will of the Father.

The Magnify 90 is a personal devotion, and we trust the Holy Spirit called us to this experience. Let us try to be unwavering in our resolve to grow in holiness. Don't let a weakness cause you anxiety; rather, offer that as a sacrifice to the Lord as well and keep trying; let Him perfect you. When we fall, let us be grateful for the opportunity to stay humble, and ask God to strengthen us as we carry on.

As the catechism passage explains, we make promises to God out of love and respect; this reflects our magnanimity. It's not a sin to slip up on the "rules" of Magnify 90, but each day we should set out striving to complete the task well. God can use weakness to bring about good. The reason we started with studying humility is because it's needed to keep us from seeking our own version of perfection. Humility helps us recall that apart from God we are nothing and can do nothing good, because He is the source of all good.

Legalistic-perfectionism is a real temptation as well, but it can be countered by a daily examination of conscience and prayers of adoration, thanksgiving, Our weaknesses give glory to God because when we turn them back over to Him, asking for the grace to do better the next time, we are assenting to the truth that He is the only one powerful enough to make us perfect. We can't do it all; remember that is trying to be something we aren't called to be is not part of magnanimity.

Consider

Have you ever struggled with perfectionism? Is there a time that letting go of your own ideas for how something should go has actually turned out to bring you closer to being a Saint? What was the hardest thing to give up this week? How are you leaning into the desert and finding joy through prayer, sacrifices, and relationships with others?

WEEKLY REFLECTIONS

Docility

St. Jane Frances de Chantal

WEEK 5-DOCILITY
St. Jane Frances de Chantal

Mortifications	S	M	T	W	T	F	S
DAILY PRAYER (30 MIN) MAGNIFICAT, LITANY, ROSARY	✝	✝	✝	✝	✝	✝	✝
DAILY MASS							
CONFESSION (MONTHLY)							
ADORATION (WEEKLY)							
NO MAKEUP			✝		✝		
MEATLESS FASTING						✝	
INTENTIONAL WALK WITH FRIEND OR HUSBAND							
CONNECT WITH PERSON WHO CAME TO MIND IN PRAYER							
OTHER:							
OTHER:							
OTHER:							

Other Daily Mortifications to Remember

- ONLY CHRISTIAN/CLASSICAL MUSIC AND PODCASTS
- ONLY RELIGIOUS PROGRAMMING IN MODERATION
- NO WEIGHING ON A SCALE
- NO SWEETS, ALCOHOL, OR SNACKS IN BETWEEN MEALS
- NO SOCIAL MEDIA
- NO UNNECESSARY SHOPPING
- _____
- _____
-

I am offering my intentions for:

- S _____
- M _____
- T _____
- W _____
- T _____
- F _____
- S _____
- Other _____

Express Use this space to journal, draw, or otherwise express your thoughts on this week's virtue. Spend some time listening to the Holy Spirit, perhaps in Adoration, and capture whatever He brings to mind or lays on your heart.

DOCILITY: DAY 29

This week we focus on docility; which, in simple terms, is being teachable.

CCC 89: There is an organic connection between our spiritual life and the dogmas. Dogmas are lights along the path of faith; they illuminate it and make it secure. Conversely, if our life is upright, our intellect and heart will be open to welcome the light shed by the dogmas of faith. (see John 8:31-32)

96: What Christ entrusted to the apostles, they in turn handed on by their preaching and writing, under the inspiration of the Holy Spirit, to all generations, until Christ returns in glory.

97: "Sacred Tradition and Sacred Scripture make up a single sacred deposit of the Word of God" (Dei Verbum 10) in which, as in a mirror, the pilgrim Church contemplates God, the source of all her riches.

98: "The Church, in her doctrine, life and worship, perpetuates and transmits to every generation all that she herself is, all that she believes" (DV 8).

"If we seek God everywhere, we find Him everywhere."
-- *St Jane Frances de Chantal*

Docile often conveys a weakness in the secular world today. Many of us may view it as an oppressive word because it's often thought to mean obedient to the point of having no convictions—such as "letting people walk all over her." But in its pure definition, docile means "willingness to be taught." It comes from the Latin *docere*, meaning "to teach," and it follows that a doctor is one who teaches and doctrine is what (s)he teaches. Dogmas are solidified teachings and connect to *docere* through the Greek *dokein* (meaning "seems good" or "suppose, think or accept") and *doxa* (meaning "common belief").

A docile person is willing to learn from a teacher. Jesus, our Divine Teacher, passed on the ability to teach to His apostles and they also had the ability to pass that teaching authority on further because of the Holy Spirit. The Word of God is recorded in Sacred Scripture and is interpreted through the authority of the Catholic Church because of Sacred Tradition. By nature of our baptism into the Body of Christ and the gifts of the Holy Spirit, we are called to be teachers, yet also teachable.

Docility fuses together our spirituality and intellect. To make the connection between our head and our heart requires we be teachable. It is a part of prudence, and practicing prudence requires us to gather information, recall our own memories, seek counsel, learn from trustworthy teachers, and prayerfully make the best choice with what we've learned in discernment.

Who are you learning from and what are you learning? Before Magnify 90 what types of media or human influences were you letting into your mind and heart? Are they still coming in? Do they teach you Truth; do they nourish your faith? Pray for docility even when it's hard to detach from worldly desires—then you'll be able to know the Truth and follow the Truth.

Who are you learning from and what are you learning? Before Magnify 90 what types of media or human influences were you letting into your mind and heart? Are they still coming in? Do they teach you Truth; do they give you faith? Pray for docility even when it's hard to detach from worldly desires—then you'll be able to know the Truth and follow the Truth.

DOCILITY: DAY 30

Reflect on this passage from the great promotor of the feminine genius, Pope St. John Paul II, calling to mind how all Christians must be docile to know our identity and our mission in Christ.

[Mission-minded] spirituality is expressed first of all by a life of complete docility to the Spirit. It commits us to being molded from within by the Spirit, so that we may become ever more like Christ. It is not possible to bear witness to Christ without reflecting his image, which is made alive in us by grace and the power of the Spirit. This docility then commits us to receive the gifts of fortitude and discernment, which are essential elements of missionary spirituality.

An example of this is found with the apostles during the Master's public life. Despite their love for him and their generous response to his call, they proved to be incapable of understanding his words and reluctant to follow him along the path of suffering and humiliation. The Spirit transformed them into courageous witnesses to Christ and enlightened heralds of his word. It was the Spirit himself who guided them along the difficult and new paths of mission.

Today, as in the past, that mission is difficult and complex, and demands the courage and light of the Spirit. We often experience the dramatic situation of the first Christian community which witnessed unbelieving and hostile forces "gathered together against the Lord and his Anointed" (Acts 4:26). Now, as then, we must pray that God will grant us boldness in preaching the Gospel; we must ponder the mysterious ways of the Spirit and allow ourselves to be led by him into all the truth (see John 16:13).

Redemptoris Missio (Pope St. John Paul II, 12/7/1990, Ch. 8, http://w2.vatican.va/content/john-paul-ii/en/encyclicals/documents/hf_jp-ii_enc_07121990_redemptoris-missio.html)

We must first know whose we are—which is to come to believe that God created us out of love. Then docility makes identity take root in our life. Following Mary's example as the Spouse of the Holy Spirit, we can form a relationship with the Holy Spirit and truly realize our shared mission as Christ's disciples. This is why Confirmation is so important! Baptism gives us the full gift of the Holy Spirit, but we are strengthened and commissioned with additional graces in Confirmation. To be docile, we must pray like Mary, who first pondered what she heard from God before acting in mission.

We need the Holy Spirit to give us clarity in our vocation, in our roles as adopted daughters of God, and boldness in our mission. If our identity is in Christ, there is no room for distractions coming from the surface level. That's where the virtues come in—they help us live in the world, without letting the wrong voices direct our path. Paraphrasing what Pope St. John Paul II wrote, the apostles couldn't get it together before Christ ascended, but after Pentecost, they were on fire!

As confirmed Catholics, we have our unique mission for spreading the Gospel in the particular way He has called us, always letting the Holy Spirit guide our actions.

What, or Who, is your identity rooted in? Of course, we all want to say Christ, but have you found yourself craving approval from others? Have you made physical appearance or fitness, your kids and their activities, a hobby or game or show, earning or saving money, or career title into your identity? If your identity is in Christ, how are you doing in your mission? Are you preaching the Good News of our Savior Jesus Christ by your way of living? How can Magnify 90 be a type of renewal for you?

DOCILITY: DAY 31

Love makes us want to be docile, but our docility also increases our desire to love God. Feminine genius St. Jane Frances De Chantal once wrote a spiritual directee that love should invite us to live virtuous lives simply for the purpose of serving God.

"Your letter showed me very clearly the state of your soul and the source of its pain and perplexity, which is your over eagerness to attain the true happiness you desire, and your lack of patience and docility to the will of Him who alone can grant it to you....It seems to me that you are not satisfied with doing those acts required for your perfection, but that you want to feel and know that you are doing them. You must put an end to that and be content with telling God, without any feeling, "Lord, with all my heart I desire to practice such and such virtue just to please You." Then, set to work, although without feeling, and lovingly resolve to serve God in this way, desiring nothing more. If you do this, you will soon find yourself in that state of tranquility and peace which is so necessary for souls who wish to live virtuously, according to the spirit, and not according to their own inclinations and judgements."
–St. Jane Frances De Chantal (Saint Francis de Sales & Jeanne Françoise Frémiot de Rabutin de Chantal. Francis de Sales, Jane de Chantal: Letters of Spiritual Direction (1988) Paulist Press)

Accordingly, prudence is said to be love, not indeed essentially, but in so far as love moves to the act of prudence. Wherefore Augustine goes on to say that "prudence is love discerning aright that which helps from that which hinders us in tending to God." Now love is said to discern because it moves the reason to discern.
- St. Thomas Aquinas, Summa Theologiae II-II Q47, a1, r1

God imprinted the desire for Him on each person's soul, though many choose to ignore or numb that desire. We are unable to purely love sacrificially like Christ, but our entire lives should be a striving to overcome our fallen nature so to find reunion with God. We know that humans can never earn Heaven, but we can certainly run in the opposite direction (toward hell) out of free will. Yes, we have the will and ability to follow our own inclinations, but we grow closer to God through our selflessness and seeking to bring God's love to others.

Augustine, as quoted by Aquinas, makes the point that we utilize prudence to figure out what will help or hurt our path to holiness. Prudence shows us how we, specific to our unique mission, are called to love—while it is Jesus' example of love that forms our prudent choices. Prudence involves our memory (which must have truth at its root), our judgements (which must be based in truth), and our action (which leads us and others to Truth). As Jesus indicated in the greatest commandment, we must love everyone like we love ourselves to be open to Heaven! To know how to love others we must be docile in allowing the Holy Spirit to guide us. We have to be really honest, and this is where we so often go wrong. How good have we gotten at lying to ourselves?

In another vein, what if there are loving choices to be made and it appears there isn't one right choice? Recall that Mary's docility to the Holy Spirit didn't automatically reveal everything to her either. She said "yes" to God out of love, but then what? From that primary mission flowed a lot of other smaller teachable moments. She pondered so much in her heart. We must follow this example.

Prudence needs not only docility, but also patience (among other minor virtues). And we know that the first thing love is, is patient (see 1 Corinthians 13:4). If we haven't yet discerned the "right things" the Holy Spirit is prompting, we wait. Sometimes the holiness is in the waiting. Let our prayer be "Lord, make your Will my will." When we are loving, we are patient. We must be teachable even if we can't see the lesson. We grow closer to Him through our open ended "Yes, Lord!" and *that* closeness is holiness

Consider

Do you do virtuous things and expect to see or feel a result? What is your reason for doing Magnify 90? Are you too comfortable in life right now? Have you asked God what He wants you to do next? Are you currently in a season of waiting? If you've been pondering something, have you considered praying a Novena of Surrender? Read 1 Peter 5:6-7 and include "As It Is In Heaven" by Phil Wickham as a part of your prayer if you want.

DOCILITY: DAY 32

St. Jane Frances de Chantal struggled against a harsh and strict personality—which is problematic when seeking to be docile. Through spiritual direction and grace, she was able to overcome her nature and become a spiritual mother to others seeking gentleness.

"As to your inward occupation with God, it could not be better. But I see you are always somewhat worrying yourself, wanting to do things that God does not want of you. When your mind is at rest near Him, ought not that to satisfy you? Does not this divine Infinity contain in itself all the sacred mysteries of Jesus and Mary? Have no desire then to seek or to know anything that God does not wish to make known to you." – *St Jane Frances de Chantal (The Spirit of Saint Jane Frances de Chantal as Shown by Her Letters (1922) Longmans, Green, and Company)*

"If someone wants to follow me, renounce self . . ." "These words are the foundation of all Christian and religious perfection. To deny self is to renounce to all the will of the flesh, all our inclinations, desires, pleasures, satisfactions, softness, tastes, humor, preferences, habits, susceptibility, aversions and repugnance to rough things; in other words, to renounce in all and for all our perverse self. Fight to destroy your character, passions and inclinations; in one word, all your nature; and this, with energetic will, with generosity, and persevering mortification of all your being." – *St Jane Frances de Chantal*

"Destroy, cut and burn all that opposes your holy will" – *St. Jane Frances de Chantal*

St. Jane Frances was a wife and mother who eventually, as a widow, started a group of religious with St. Francis de Sales. She had an austere personality that had to be overcome because she was too perfectionistic with respect to checking off boxes and achieving "human" successes in the spiritual realm. St. Francis taught her that it was better to be open to God's will, letting nothing trouble her—even interruptions to her prayer or having to adjust her plans to better align with openness to God's will. He taught her to let everything come to her as an opportunity to show love and mercy. She learned to magnify the Lord through her feminine genius. She became very gentle in her dealings with others—though that wasn't her natural way. She even had to learn to be gentle with herself. St. Francis de Sales encouraged her to be less attached to "perfect" mortifications and more concerned with her ability to seek God's will in her prayer.

For us, this may mean eating a snack when we are nursing a baby even if we wanted to fast. This may mean eating meat on a Friday if we are at a dinner party and it's being served by our gracious host. It may also mean having to stay up later caring for a sick dependent, and then when we find ourselves oversleeping in the morning, still getting in our prayer time and asking God to give us the grace to be gentle with our human nature. We aren't going to be perfect, but we can offer Him even that. So perhaps, when we have eaten meat on a meatless day or hit snooze 3 times, we can offer a different fast, such as fasting from flavorful additions to our food or going about our day smiling even when we are tired. Overcoming frustration, worry, or inclination to a temper are probably even more meaningful mortifications to God—all of which require us to practice docility.

Gentleness is a key piece of docility. Nothing should cause us to despair or fear, even our own defaults. We, first and foremost, have to be gentle with ourselves. When we see places where we need to do better, where we need to grow, and the virtues we need to practice more, these should be causes of joy, not discouragement! We should be humbly joyful that God has brought to light places where He wishes us to grow. Our docility keeps us trying, and trying again to be the Saints only He can perfect us into. We must ask God to refine us. We cooperate in that as we mortify our desires for anything that separates us from the will of God. Being in the presence of God should be the root from which everything else in our life flows. Our prayers should be that He takes away the temptations we have to oppose His perfect will.

Do you ever concern yourself with others as a way to avoid looking at your own interior life? It's good to care about others, but not to the exclusion of the work that needs to be done in your soul. Is your life indicative of docility to the Holy Spirit? What current struggles against docility are you fighting? Have you asked God for help? Can a change in your lifestyle help? Sometimes we can be too harsh as well. Is God asking you to be gentle with yourself or others?

DOCILITY: DAY 33

Reflect on how we come to know the Truth, and how it is transmitted.

CCC 84: The apostles entrusted the "Sacred deposit" of the faith (the depositum fidei), contained in Sacred Scripture and Tradition, to the whole of the Church. "By adhering to [this heritage] the entire holy people, united to its pastors, remains always faithful to the teaching of the apostles, to the brotherhood, to the breaking of bread and the prayers. So, in maintaining, practicing and professing the faith that has been handed on, there should be a remarkable harmony between the bishops and the faithful."

86: Yet this Magisterium is not superior to the Word of God, but is its servant. It teaches only what has been handed on to it. At the divine command and with the help of the Holy Spirit, it listens to this devotedly, guards it with dedication and expounds it faithfully. All that it proposes for belief as being divinely revealed is drawn from this single deposit of faith." (DV 20)

But you, beloved, remember the words spoken beforehand by the apostles of our Lord Jesus Christ, for they told you, "In [the] last time there will be scoffers who will live according to their own godless desires." These are the ones who cause divisions; they live on the natural plane, devoid of the Spirit. But you, beloved, build yourselves up in your most holy faith; pray in the Holy Spirit. Keep yourselves in the love of God and wait for the mercy of our Lord Jesus Christ that leads to eternal life.
– Jude 17-21

We either believe the Truth exists or we don't. If nothing is true, then everything is "true"—and what's the point of that kind of existence? We can feel it in our hearts, we are created for some purpose. Social media and the news would make it seem that people in our world thrive according to their own whims and desires. This is in stark contrast to what God asks people to do. We can't just make up our own reason for living: the reason is God. We also can't interpret the Bible any way that we want to fit the human desires we have. We can't make religious practices or rituals based on an opinion.

We are not left alone to figure things out. Jesus told the Apostles that He would send them a Helper after He ascended into Heaven. He told them that the Holy Spirit would guide them into the Truth, and Jesus also gave the Apostles the ability to pass that revealed Truth on in His name. They used the authority given to them to teach others how to be teachers. So teachers begin first as disciples.

The Church is docile herself, because She's always receptive to the promptings of the Holy Spirit, illuminating the path toward Heaven like a lighthouse. Although various groups have left the Church in protest of challenging teachings or bad human leaders, and some humans have fallen into very grave sin while working for the Church, the passage from Jude tells us that those who cause divisions are devoid of the Spirit.

The Spirit is leading the Church, so we must always trust that the gates of hell won't prevail! We must have unity, and that means there can't be a bunch of opinions telling us what is "true." We can't pick and choose what teachings we believe. Disunity takes away from fully glorifying Him. We need a unified approach to interpreting the Bible, worshiping God, and living in the world while not being attached to it. It's found in the church begun by Jesus: The Catholic Church.

Consider

Is there a Church teaching you struggle with? Find out why it's taught, then pray, and then trust. How has your life journey brought you to where you are now in your faith story? How has docility to the Catholic Church's teachings been a source of peace and freedom in your life? Have you seen a benefit to fasting as you pursue virtue? What connection do you see between fasting and docility?

DOCILITY: DAY 34

As children, grafted into the Body of Christ, we have to listen to our Father. He will always draw us closer to Him through our docility.

For those who are led by the Spirit of God are children of God. For you did not receive a spirit of slavery to fall back into fear, but you received a spirit of adoption, through which we cry, "Abba, Father!" The Spirit itself bears witness with our spirit that we are children of God, and if children, then heirs, heirs of God and joint heirs with Christ, if only we suffer with him so that we may also be glorified with him.
– *Romans 8:14-17*

"In prayer, more is accomplished by listening than by talking." – *often attributed to both St. Francis de Sales and St. Jane Frances de Chantal*

Being adopted children of God is even better than being biological children of God. In the time of St. Paul writing, Roman people could give up a biological child for a variety of reasons, but once adopted, a child was in the family permanently. Being a truly adopted child comes with all the benefits of family life and love and we can't be discarded (we can certainly walk away from the family though)! Through the Holy Spirit we come to have life with God as His daughters. This doesn't mean things on Earth will be easy; suffering is part of the arrangement if we want to be glorified, as exemplified in Christ's Passion. We can't expect Heaven without the cross.

The mortifications of Magnify 90 are too difficult to do alone, but we don't have to! Of course we have the other women in the desert with us—but we also have the Paraclete, the Holy Spirit! Just as Jesus was in the desert to overcome sin (for us, not Himself, of course), so too are we called to be led by the Holy Spirit in our own deserts.

Through humility we can recognize that we don't know how to truly commune with God after all; we need help. We have a powerful intercessor in the Holy Spirit, helping to keep our prayer in line with God's will. Being docile to the Holy Spirit teaches us how to pray. We can't forget to ask the Holy Spirit to show us what to do in a certain moment, or what to say during a conversation, or where to go when we are more than just physically lost. More than anything, may the Holy Spirit open our minds and hearts to make good confessions so that we stay in union with God.

Consider

Breathe "Come Holy Spirit" statements throughout the day when you feel your peace shaken—driving in traffic, waiting in line at the check-out, folding 14 loads of laundry, seeing kid's toys everywhere, finishing up a work project on the weekend. Ask for the Holy Spirit to guide you into the Truth, to pray on your behalf, and to keep you calm. Make "Holy Spirit" by Francesca Battistelli a part of your prayer today.

This week of docility is a wonderful time to receive the Sacrament of Reconciliation as you recognize times when you've tried to be self-reliant. Consider how truly teachable you have been since the Magnify 90 began. Have you been fighting tooth and nail against the self-denial or against the increased spiritual practices? Thank you for staying with it, sister!

DOCILITY: DAY 35

The docility of women shows others, including men, what it means to be free in the spiritual sense. We have the greatest impact on others' pursuits of virtue when we live out our fiat as Mary's openness revealed the feminine genius for us.

And the angel said to her in reply, "The Holy Spirit will come upon you, and the power of the Most High will overshadow you. Therefore the child to be born will be called holy, the Son of God. And behold, Elizabeth, your relative, has also conceived a son in her old age, and this is the sixth month for her who was called barren; for nothing will be impossible for God. Mary said, "Behold, I am the handmaid of the Lord. May it be done to me according to your word." Then the angel departed from her. – *Luke 1:35-38*

"A person who has this true freedom will leave her prayer, unruffled, gracious toward the person who has unexpectedly disturbed her, for to her it's all the same—serving God by meditating or serving Him by responding to her neighbor. Both are the will of God, but helping the neighbor is necessary at that particular moment. We have occasion to practice this freedom whenever things don't go the way we'd like them to; for anyone who is not attached to her own ways will not get impatient when things go otherwise." – *St. Francis de Sales to St. Jane Frances de Chantal (Saint Francis de Sales & Jeanne Françoise Frémiot de Rabutin de Chantal. Francis de Sales, Jane de Chantal: Letters of Spiritual Direction (1988) Paulist Press)*

"Spirit of life, by whose power the Word was made flesh in the womb of the Virgin Mary, the woman of attentive silence, make us docile to the promptings of your love and ever ready to accept the signs of the times which you place along the paths of history. Come, Spirit of love and peace!"
– *St. John Paul II, Come Spirit of Love and Peace! (1998)*

As Mary *received* the most shocking news of her life, she was *sensitive* to what it meant. She was *generous* in her response, and she *brought forth* Christ into the world. The prototype of the feminine genius spirituality, Mary cooperated with God's salvific plan for all of humanity! What an amazing trailblazer for us modern women. Let us seek to follow her example, aware that we don't have to fit the mold of what the world tells us we should do. Let us be open to the Holy Spirit through prayer and the grace given in the sacraments. This is where freedom to love comes from—the ability to detach from vices, selfishness, and sins.

Docility helps find the ability to say no to temptation. When we are confined by something of this world, we aren't truly free.

St. Jane Frances de Chantal received a letter from St. Francis de Sales that encouraged her to be free from even attachment to her plans. As we read earlier this week, it wasn't in her nature to be docile, but she practiced it. She wasn't the only one that benefited from her freedom and virtue. The example of their mother overcoming her natural tendencies showed her children that holiness stems from the willingness to let God move in us.

If we have children in our care, through our vocation or profession or volunteering or extended family, we must be conscious of their eyes watching the way we pursue virtue. This includes adults who are still yet spiritual children. What we do matters even more than what we say. This is especially obvious in our participation at Mass. When teachers and parents seem to begrudgingly go to Mass, have a blank stare and unfolded hands, don't bother to alter their posture, and perhaps even complain about the length of Mass or the homily, are not helping children to grow in reverence of the Lord. When children see the adult influences in their life excited about the gift of the Mass and are taught about the beauty, history, and meaning of the Mass, they are more likely to put into practice the virtue of gratitude for God's sacrifice and grace. Young children are still teachable, still naturally docile—most of them haven't yet put up the walls of self-reliance, so we must start encouraging them in their faith at younger ages by living our own faith boldly.

Consider

Reflect on the past week. See what preoccupations you have and offer those to the Lord in prayer. Where have you been receptive, sensitive, generous, and maternal (in the sense of bearing Christ to others)? Is there an experience of docility to be joyful for? Did you have an occasion when you didn't listen to the promptings of the Holy Spirit? How has your participation in the Mass given witness to it being the closest we can get to Heaven while on Earth? Include "Hail Mary – Gentle Woman" in your prayer today.

WEEKLY REFLECTIONS

Industriousness

St. Katharine Drexel

WEEK 6-INDUSTRIOUSNESS
St. Katharine Drexel

Mortifications	S	M	T	W	T	F	S
DAILY PRAYER (30 MIN) MAGNIFICAT, LITANY, ROSARY	✝	✝	✝	✝	✝	✝	✝
DAILY MASS							
CONFESSION (MONTHLY)							
ADORATION (WEEKLY)							
NO MAKEUP			✝			✝	
MEATLESS FASTING						✝	
INTENTIONAL WALK WITH FRIEND OR HUSBAND							
CONNECT WITH PERSON WHO CAME TO MIND IN PRAYER							
OTHER:							
OTHER:							
OTHER:							

Other Daily Mortifications to Remember

- ONLY CHRISTIAN/CLASSICAL MUSIC AND PODCASTS
- ONLY RELIGIOUS PROGRAMMING IN MODERATION
- NO WEIGHING ON A SCALE
- NO SWEETS, ALCOHOL, OR SNACKS IN BETWEEN MEALS
- NO SOCIAL MEDIA
- NO UNNECESSARY SHOPPING
- _____
- _____
- _____

I am offering my intentions for:

S ● _____
M ● _____
T ● _____
W ● _____
T ● _____
F ● _____
S ● _____
Other ● _____

Express Use this space to journal, draw, or otherwise express your thoughts on this week's virtue. Spend some time listening to the Holy Spirit, perhaps in Adoration, and capture whatever He brings to mind or lays on your heart.

INDUSTRIOUSNESS: DAY 36

DAY 36: Magnify 90 is an opportunity to practice asceticism, which needs the virtue of industriousness, the theme for this week. Consider the definition of asceticism:

Spiritual effort or exercise in the pursuit of virtue. The purpose is to grow in Christian perfection. Its principles and norms are expanded in ascetical theology. (Etymology: Greek *askētikos*, literally, given to exercise; industrious; applied to hermits who strictly exercised themselves in religious devotion.) *(Hardon, J. Pocket Catholic Dictionary (1985) Image Books)*

Industriousness is a virtue under fortitude; it is diligence in human work that leads to spiritual maturity. It helps us learn not to be distracted from our goal of sainthood, despite the many worldly temptations to focus on the present. These ninety days are devoted to emptying ourselves so that our thirst for God allows Him to fill us with virtue. We must participate in this process. We must exert effort in pursuing virtue.

"Work" is *exerting some energy with a purpose in mind, seeking a specific result.* Even people of no religion see the need for human fulfillment through creating something, intellectually or tangibly. Within the Catholic Church, though, we see the fullness of purpose in work; that is, to continue God's creativity. So, every time Christians exert our energy, we must seek to have the purest goal of honoring God. This is how we industriously magnify the Lord; staying near Him in a personal relationship through prayer that then begets loving action. That's why we flow from docility to industriousness in our learning about the virtues. We must have the right pattern of prayer and interior to active and exterior movements in our lives.

We were created out of God's love and meant to live eternally with Him forever, should we choose to freely love Him back. God gives us many means to see His goodness and many opportunities to participate in His Divine Nature that help us live out our choice to love Him. Participating in His creative work is one of those ways. For women it most often manifests itself in being receptive to children and being the heart of the family. There are married women who are unable to have children physically (ever, or any longer), and this is certainly a heavy cross to bear. Adoption and foster-parenting are frequent vocational calls from the Lord. But it may be the case that a wife and husband discern that not to be their vocation. A woman may be called to work industriously in the world while bearing Christ's light as a spiritual mother to many that physical motherhood could prevent her from being. Should her vocational call be to consecrated religious life, she sacrifices a family of her own to bring Glory to God through contemplation and serving others in the community at large. Some women are called to remain single, yet consecrated to Christ, living in the world. They are women who can work industriously in their careers, sharing the gospel in ways and places religious are not typically present. Women may volunteer in philanthropic endeavors beyond their day job, with or without families, or they may be called to specific missionary lifestyles as well, where spiritual motherhood calls abound. Life is an opportunity to be joyful in working hard as guardians for the vocation God gave us.

All of these vocations are opportunities for sanctification by dying to our own personal desires. We may *want* to have a job that pays well, but if we stay close to God in prayer, we may sense Him calling us to something else. Choosing to *not* listen to that goes against His will and won't lead to eternal happiness. We may want a family, but if God is asking us to enter religious life or become a consecrated lay woman, we must listen to Him. Some of us may want to change what we are currently doing, but discernment is vital. *If* we hear God calling us to make a change, He will bring good out of our willingness. The sacrifices we make to participate fully in His creative work are steps along the path to Heaven. Industriousness finds a home in all women's pursuit of virtue, no matter her state in life, because we must not quit when the work that we are asked to do for God's glory gets hard.

How is your spiritual effort, weeks into *Magnify*? Do you pray about your work and how you go about it? Do you make choices in your work that go against the dignity of another? How do you respond to God's Will if it conflicts with your expectations or your desire to live up to world's expectations? Read CCC 307 and 323 for further meditation.

INDUSTRIOUSNESS: DAY 37

Rooting our industriousness in silence, prayer, and the sacraments is necessary to avoid becoming spiritual "perfectionists" who become blinded by success and lose our sense of docility.

When he returned to his disciples, he found them asleep. He said to Peter, "So you could not keep watch with me for one hour? Watch and pray that you may not undergo the test. The spirit is willing, but the flesh is weak."
– *Matthew 26:40-41*

They that hope in the LORD will renew their strength, they will soar on eagles' wings; they will run and not grow weary, walk and not grow faint.
– *Isaiah 40:31*

"The active life, to be productive, must have contemplation. When it gets to a certain height, it overflows to active life, and gets help and strength from the heart of God."
– *St. Katharine Drexel (from the St. Katharine Drexel Mission Center & National Shrine Novena)*

"The patient and humble endurance of the cross, whatever nature it may be, is the highest work we have to do." – *St. Katharine Drexel*

Others count on our contributions. Depending on our state in life, goals and deadlines must be met, kids cared for, meetings attended, valuations of time management and tough choices made. We need a virtue that helps us work hard to do God's will for our life. Industriousness is a virtue opposed to sinful inaction. The Bible is full of passages condemning laziness, fearful trepidation, and inaction when we are called to act. We certainly can't do it all, but it's virtuous to be diligent at school, at home, at work, and everywhere docility to God's will calls us.

Industriousness can only be virtuous if we balance it with humility and charity. We can acknowledge prayer and our sacramental relationship with God as the source of strength, so that we can magnify the Lord by our commitment to hard work. We can't focus on praise we may receive or not receive from others. Our achievements should always point to God. Worldly industriousness will lead us into the sin of pride.

Why do we get stuck so deeply on doing a certain task at a certain time? Why are we volunteering our time while our family balance suffers? Why we are in a specific career field that destroys our spirituality? Are we overcommitted? Are we hiding behind attachments that keep us from building relationships with others, encountering the needy (they may be our own children!), or donating time to church needs? Do we trust Him to give us the energy necessary to run the course that leads us to sainthood? At various stages of our lives, the answers to these questions may be different.

We rightly order our day by starting with prayer and prioritizing Jesus and the Eucharist. We lean on Him, realizing that Christ in us accomplishes the good. We should never want to get in the way with our own fears of tiredness, though.

When we find ourselves exhausted and run ragged, we need to dwell in Christ's love. As St. Katharine Drexel said, to have a productive active life, we must have contemplation, and then the active life flows through God appropriately. It is a balance of periods of rest and periods of action. We must rest upon the Sacred Heart of Jesus first, then love our neighbor. Let us come to the Lord in confession for the times we've been self-reliant or the times we've been spiritually apathetic and ask for strength to bring glory to Him through the work that we do.

 *Consider*

Can you be virtuously industrious if you don't know God's will? Where can you give more silence for God to speak to you? Are you afraid to do something God laid on your heart for fear that it will be too hard or take too much energy away from something you like to do better? If you want, include "My Revival" by Lauren Daigle as part of your prayer today.

INDUSTRIOUSNESS: DAY 38

St. Katharine reminds us that joy is vital to a Christian woman's successful work, and whatever work we do must be worthy of the name of the Lord on our soul.

"If we wish to serve God and love our neighbor well, we must manifest our joy in the service we render to him and them. Let us open wide our hearts. It is joy which invites us to press forward and fear nothing." – *St. Katharine Drexel (USCCB. Open Wide Our Hearts (2018) http://www.usccb.org/issues-and-action/human-life-and-dignity/racism/upload/open-wide-our-hearts.pdf)*

"Always try to approach the holy table with more and more love. Divest your heart of all love of the world and of yourself and then you will leave room for Jesus. Thank Our Lord for having redeemed your soul with His Most Precious Blood." – *St. Katharine Drexel (Cheryl D. Hughes. Katharine Drexel: The Riches-to-Rags Life Story of an American Catholic Saint (2014) Wm. B. Eerdmans Publishing)*

Let the word of Christ dwell in you richly, as in all wisdom you teach and admonish one another, singing psalms, hymns, and spiritual songs with gratitude in your hearts to God. And whatever you do, in word or in deed, do everything in the name of the Lord Jesus, giving thanks to God the Father through him.
– Colossians 3:16-17

St. Katharine Drexel was an American woman with substantial financial means; the family's estate, in current dollars, would have been worth nearly $250 million. She was magnanimous in wanting to bring God glory, and she worked industriously because she was docile to the Spirit's promptings. She was a true feminine genius that had a spirituality of self-emptying so that her hunger was always for the Lord. She trusted that God always provides for the work that He wants done.

St. Katharine felt a desire to be a cloistered nun, especially so she could receive the Eucharist more frequently, but also saw all the people needing tangible love and was concerned that someone should do something about it. She was able to speak with Pope Leo XIII about her concern for Native Americans and African Americans and asked him to send missionaries. He told *her* to be the missionary.

St. Katharine started an order specifically to magnify the Lord to Native Americans and African Americans in the very challenging and often anti-Catholic post-Civil War era. She lived out her vocation industriously until the 1950s. The Sisters of the Blessed Sacrament charism is rooted in contemplative prayer, particularly the Eucharist; yet through that deep connection to the Lord they joyfully serve Him and others, working actively in the world.

Katharine gave up a comfortable life to bring Christ to others. She had joy in doing this, despite ridicule, persecution, and a threat of being tarred and feathered! She knew her identity was in Christ and her mission was love. Every feminine genius should be able to say this.

Our work, in or out of the home, may lead to unhappiness and/or sin if we place our need for human approval and comfort over desiring Heaven. We do not need a promotion or raise to be worthy of Heaven. We do not need a social media post to acknowledge the meaningful work we do in the home. We do not need to spend money on keeping up "living the American dream" appearances or frivolous comforts. We let our praise be of God.

 **Have you ever specifically asked God what work He wants you to do? Do changes need to happen in your career or home management to bring joyful pursuit of sainthood as the goal? What is your identity and mission?**

If St. Katharine's story caught your interest, read more about her. Consider both *Katharine Drexel: The Riches-to-Rags Story of an American Catholic Saint* by Cheryl C.D. Hughes (Wm. B. Eerdmans, 2014) and *Saint Katharine: The Life of Katharine Drexel* by Cordelia Frances Biddle (Westholme Publishing, 2014).

INDUSTRIOUSNESS: DAY 39

One of work's rightly ordered goals is to care for others. Storing away excess of goods or money while others go without basic needs for dignity is not compatible with Jesus' instruction. In the same virtue, we must take care to uphold the dignity of others by not enabling or belittling them either.

In every way I have shown you that by hard work of that sort we must help the weak, and keep in mind the words of the Lord Jesus who himself said, 'It is more blessed to give than to receive.' – *Acts 20:35*

CCC 2426: The development of economic activity and growth in production are meant to provide for the needs of human beings. Economic life is not meant solely to multiply goods produced and increase profit or power; it is ordered first of all to the service of persons, of the whole man, and of the entire human community. Economic activity, conducted according to its own proper methods, is to be exercised within the limits of the moral order, in keeping with social justice so as to correspond to God's plan for man. (GS 64)

2444: "The Church's love for the poor . . . is a part of her constant tradition." This love is inspired by the Gospel of the Beatitudes, of the poverty of Jesus, and of his concern for the poor. (CA 57) Love for the poor is even one of the motives for the duty of working so as to "be able to give to those in need." (Ephesians 4:28) It extends not only to material poverty but also to the many forms of cultural and religious poverty. (CA 57)

Many of us may try to connect our work (both paid and unpaid) to our vocation, yet we struggle to find a relationship with God in the secular atmosphere. The culture defines us and our value by what we do, especially the work's monetary value. So those without a lot of money are generally underrepresented, devalued, and brushed aside. Stay-at-home moms and wives, and working moms, single women or religiously consecrated, retirees: we all matter. So long as we live for God to be magnified through whatever work we do, we are becoming Saints.

This means work is not for work's sake. It should bring the whole human race closer to God. Not only do we have to work to serve the poor and forgotten physically, we need to serve the spiritually poor, too. This can be done in the workplace or through our work in the home. Our feminine genius allows us to be receptive to the needs of others and our industriousness helps us to answer the call. If we are in a position of power, God has trusted us with the well-being of those we manage or care for. We cannot force people, we cannot control or threaten them. We utilize sensitively to inspire others and invite them to work hard, leading by positive example whether as a mom or manager, as an employee, or as a student. We should start each day fresh, seeking to give more than we get, and at night, judge our day's hard work by its output of Christ-like behavior, strategies, and conversation.

Consider

How does industriousness in your life pass on dignity to others? How do you share your faith and your comforts? What hard things has God asked you to do for others through your work, both paid and unpaid, and how has it helped you find joy in sacrifice?

INDUSTRIOUSNESS: DAY 40

Mortifications help us to be industrious as well—it removes our attachments that inhibit working hard to magnify God's glory. We focus on the Eucharist as our source of comfort.

"Often in my desire to work for others I find my hands tied; something hinders my charitable designs, some hostile influence renders me powerless, my prayers seem to avail nothing, my kind acts are rejected, I seem to do wrong things when I'm trying to do my best. In such cases I must not grieve—I am only treading in my master steps." – *St. Katharine Drexel (from the St. Katharine Drexel Mission Center & National Shrine Novena)*

"In Holy Communion the life of God in a particular way is imparted to my soul. It is there that God becomes the soul of my soul, to do, to suffer all for the love of Him who died for me, and if Thou art for me, if Thou art within me, what can I fear, O, My God?" – *St. Katharine Drexel (Cheryl D. Hughes. Katharine Drexel: The Riches-to-Rags Life Story of an American Catholic Saint (2014) Wm. B. Eerdmans Publishing)*

Do not work for food that perishes but for the food that endures for eternal life, which the Son of Man will give you. For on him the Father, God, has set his seal. – *John 6: 27*

When we are industrious for the glory of God, we will not often find the road easy. We come across financial or logistical hardships, we get sick, people give us a hard time or don't understand us, people don't want the help we try to offer, our prayers seem fruitless…the list of ways that our gift of love can be derailed are endless. This does not necessarily mean we are doing something wrong. If we have prayed, discerned, and tried to listen to the Holy Spirit without our own pride getting in the way, we can't despair. St. Katharine encourages us to recognize that we are walking with God—because Jesus' steps were met with worldly resistance as well.

In times of apparent ineffectiveness, reflect on Mary's feelings at the foot of the cross. She bore God's very life into this world; yet, in that moment, her heart was pierced. She knows our struggle to work hard and do good in God's vineyard, yet feel unable, unworthy, or unsure. Pray the following prayer that's been attributed to St. Katharine Drexel's writings, but is actually one she copied down from a little book of Marian reflections and devotions.

Oh Mary, make me endeavor, by all the means in my power, to extend the kingdom of your divine son and offer incessantly my prayers for the conversion of those who are yet in darkness or estranged from his fold. (Very Rev. Peter Kenrick. *The Month of May* (1841) C Dolman London)

The key to continuing on the path of pious hard work is grace. Because industriousness is a part of fortitude, we can be sure that we need fortification for the hard work asked of us as co-creators. What better food for the journey is there than the Bread of Life and the Living Water?

 **Consider**

When have you tried to serve others only to be rejected? How has Eucharistic Adoration given you consolation and patience? In what ways can you foster a deeper Eucharistic amazement? Has the Rosary or other Marian devotions strengthened your love for the Body and Blood of Christ?

INDUSTRIOUSNESS: DAY 41

The diligence with which we try to love God and love others is where our work matters, no matter our charism or vocational call.

Avoid profane and silly myths. Train yourself for devotion, for, while physical training is of limited value, devotion is valuable in every respect, since it holds a promise of life both for the present and for the future. This saying is trustworthy and deserves full acceptance. For this we toil and struggle, because we have set our hope on the living God, who is the savior of all, especially of those who believe.
– 1 Timothy 4:7-10

For this very reason, make every effort to supplement your faith with virtue, virtue with knowledge, knowledge with self-control, self-control with endurance, endurance with devotion, devotion with mutual affection, mutual affection with love. If these are yours and increase in abundance, they will keep you from being idle or unfruitful in the knowledge of our Lord Jesus Christ. *– 2 Peter 1:5-8*

CCC 2407: In economic matters, respect for human dignity requires the practice of the virtue of temperance, so as to moderate attachment to this world's goods; the practice of the virtue of justice, to preserve our neighbor's rights and render him what is his due; and the practice of solidarity, in accordance with the golden rule and in keeping with the generosity of the Lord, who "though he was rich, yet for your sake . . . became poor so that by his poverty, you might become rich. (2 Corinthians 8:9)"

To grow in love, 2 Peter says, is to avoid idleness. And as 1 Timothy says, we must train for devotion. Training to be a saint is not passive! There are many crosses to bear and many attachments to die to if we are truly thirsting for God. And thankfully, there are many spiritual consolations and joyful blessings received as God shows mercy and everlasting faithfulness to us. He will never lead us wrong. He knows what we need, and the work He calls us to is part of our sanctification process.

If we look at 1 Timothy 4 *with* 2 Peter 1, we can see connections between growth in virtue and deepening devotion to the Lord. Asceticism is an important piece of growth in virtue. Asceticism and denying ourselves little comforts help us practice the fortitude necessary to say "no" when sinful temptations come our way. Working hard even when we don't feel like it, or despite contrary conditions, aids us in developing the necessary strength to be diligent in spiritual work as well. Mortifying our attachments to material comforts or inordinate bodily desires also helps our solidarity with those around the world who go without so many things we may be used to. We are less distracted by the world and all of the Evil One's temptations when we are focused on working for God's glory. Solidarity provides an opportunity for unity that forces the devil out.

Dying to ourselves means we have the opportunity to rise with Him. When we let life float easily by, we fall into loving ourselves much more than God and others. As the Catechism passage reminds us, riches and worldly goods must only be taken and used as a blessing to bring Christ to others.

Secular industry is focused on productiveness, but as a virtue, industriousness is concerned with working hard to fulfill the commandment to love our neighbor as ourselves, so as to bring God glory. Our productivity must truly be wrapped up in how diligently we love God and people.

What are you training for? How do you supplement your faith? Does offering up a cross make it a little lighter to bear? Has any mortification made in these past weeks helped you feel solidarity with those people that involuntarily go without things we take for granted?

INDUSTRIOUSNESS: DAY 42

Sundays are a day of rest, of "*re-creation*." Industriousness isn't about working constantly. There must be time for prayer and leisure that reminds us of the goodness of God.

CCC 2185: On Sundays and other holy days of obligation, the faithful are to refrain from engaging in work or activities that hinder the worship owed to God, the joy proper to the Lord's Day, the performance of the works of mercy, and the appropriate relaxation of mind and body. (Code of Canon Law 120) Family needs or important social service can legitimately excuse from the obligation of Sunday rest. The faithful should see to it that legitimate excuses do not lead to habits prejudicial to religion, family life, and health. "The charity of truth seeks holy leisure- the necessity of charity accepts just work." (St. Augustine)

2186: Those Christians who have leisure should be mindful of their brethren who have the same needs and the same rights, yet cannot rest from work because of poverty and misery. Sunday is traditionally consecrated by Christian piety to good works and humble service of the sick, the infirm, and the elderly. Christians will also sanctify Sunday by devoting time and care to their families and relatives, often difficult to do on other days of the week. Sunday is a time for reflection, silence, cultivation of the mind, and meditation which furthers the growth of the Christian interior life.

We can't discuss industriousness without reflecting on holy leisure. Hard physical work should be suspended to observe the Holy Days of God. Jesus said the Sabbath was created for man, not man for the Sabbath—just as work was created for man, not man for work. God knows what we need to grow in holiness, and thus He gave us work and rest. We need a time for rejuvenating our bodies and spirits so that we can continue on working diligently to bring Him honor. We must take time to focus on God's goodness undistracted by the ways of the world. We live in it, but we aren't made to be attached to it. To remind us of that, can we step away from worldly commitments for a day? This rhythm of life sanctifies us.

Sundays remind us of what we need. We need our Eucharistic Lord. We need true, in-person community. We need love. We need healthy food and water. We need shelter and rest. We remember *Whose* we are through enjoying nature, playing with children, taking a nap, eating dinner with friends, but most especially taking time to worship the Lord at Sunday Mass.

The mortifications of Magnify 90 are to help us detach, but a lessening of the fasts on Sunday may remind us that we have hope for eternal happiness. Things we've given up are not needed to become Saints, but they may refresh us a little as we celebrate Easter in a smaller way each Sunday because Jesus has triumphed over death! Being humbly honest we will see that we don't need 24/7 news, social media, alcohol, sweets, make-up, and we certainly don't need to be defined by a number on the scale, nor do we need accessories and beautiful clothes. These may be helpful and beneficial when rightly ordered, but they are not necessary.

Relaxation is *not an excuse to sin*. Whenever we take time for rest, we don't just let our virtues go. Debauchery, drunkenness, gluttony, trashy TV, perverted movies, lustful behaviors, gossipy chats… these are never okay, not even on our "off" day. The fact that we were "good" all week does not give us a free pass. A sin is a sin, whenever it happens.

Consider

Have you used recreation or leisure as an excuse to neglect your practice of virtue? How can you magnify the Lord even through creation and recreation? How can you use rest and leisure as an opportunity to grow in holiness? If you'd like, include "Add to the Beauty" by Sara Groves as a part of your prayer.

WEEKLY REFLECTIONS

Purity & Modesty

St. Lucy, St. Clare &
Our Lady of Fatima

WEEK 7-PURITY & MODESTY
St. Lucy, St. Clare, & Our Lady of Fatima

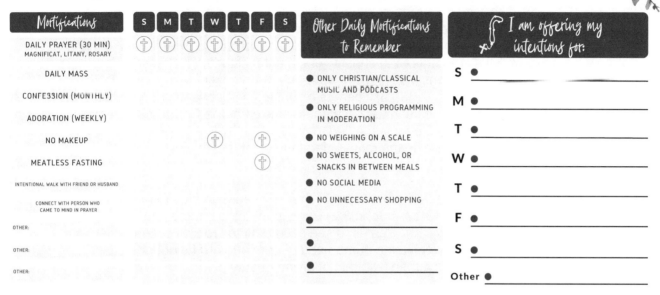

Mortifications	S	M	T	W	T	F	S
DAILY PRAYER (30 MIN) MAGNIFICAT, LITANY, ROSARY	✝	✝	✝	✝	✝	✝	✝
DAILY MASS							
CONFESSION (MONTHLY)							
ADORATION (WEEKLY)							
NO MAKEUP			✝			✝	
MEATLESS FASTING						✝	
INTENTIONAL WALK WITH FRIEND OR HUSBAND							
CONNECT WITH PERSON WHO CAME TO MIND IN PRAYER							
OTHER:							
OTHER:							
OTHER:							

Other Daily Mortifications to Remember

- ONLY CHRISTIAN/CLASSICAL MUSIC AND PODCASTS
- ONLY RELIGIOUS PROGRAMMING IN MODERATION
- NO WEIGHING ON A SCALE
- NO SWEETS, ALCOHOL, OR SNACKS IN BETWEEN MEALS
- NO SOCIAL MEDIA
- NO UNNECESSARY SHOPPING
- _____
- _____
- _____

I am offering my intentions for:

- S _____
- M _____
- T _____
- W _____
- T _____
- F _____
- S _____
- Other _____

Express Use this space to journal, draw, or otherwise express your thoughts on this week's virtue. Spend some time listening to the Holy Spirit, perhaps in Adoration, and capture whatever He brings to mind or lays on your heart.

PURITY & MODESTY: DAY 43

The virtue of purity influences the virtue of modesty, and although the two may be interchanged in everyday conversation, they have differences. We must practice both as we seek to magnify the Lord like Mary.

CCC 2518: The sixth beatitude proclaims, "Blessed are the pure in heart, for they shall see God." (Matt 5:8) "Pure in heart" refers to those who have attuned their intellects and wills to the demands of God's holiness, chiefly in three areas: charity; (1 Timothy 4:3-9; 2 Timothy 2:22) chastity or sexual rectitude; (1 Thessalonians 4:7; Colossians 3:5; Ephesians 4:19) love of truth and orthodoxy of faith. (Titus 1:15; 1 Timothy 1:3-4; 2 Timothy 2:23-26) There is a connection between purity of heart, of body, and of faith: The faithful must believe the articles of the Creed "so that by believing they may obey God, by obeying may live well, by living well may purify their hearts, and with pure hearts may understand what they believe." (St. Augustine)

2519: The "pure in heart" are promised that they will see God face to face and be like him. (1 Corinthians 13:12; 1 John 3:2) Purity of heart is the precondition of the vision of God. Even now it enables us to see according to God, to accept others as "neighbors"; it lets us perceive the human body - ours and our neighbor's - as a temple of the Holy Spirit, a manifestation of divine beauty.

Women pure in heart and modest in deed model the virtue of <u>justice</u> toward others and honor God, which is to be charitable. Some nuanced differences between the two topics of this week: to be modest is to make <u>prudent</u> choices regarding our appearance and our behavior. Being pure of heart takes <u>fortitude</u> to resist the temptations to assimilate into modern culture for the sake of fitting in, and <u>temperance</u> to moderate our thoughts, our desires, and our attitudes. One could live out modesty without having a pure heart. We can see that having the virtue of purity and modesty draws upon all of the cardinal virtues!

Perhaps the word modesty makes some women uncomfortable because of the culture they were raised in. But we shouldn't look at modesty like something that restricts our sense of style or is unfairly burdensome given modern clothing options. This week strive to see that modesty would be truly reflective of a pure heart—one that desires the highest good (Heaven) for all and never wishes to magnify anything other than Jesus. Modesty is not really about what we can't wear; it's about the desires of our heart and the souls of others that we are called to treasure. If we value God dwelling in our soul as His daughters, our outward appearance will be reflective of this.

We can let our unique personalities and tastes shine externally, but in desiring to be a Saint, our soul and body must point others and ourselves to God. If we are seeking to let God be what people see when they look at us, then we will certainly find ourselves less concerned with fashion and an appearance-driven need for approval. We do need to take care of ourselves and not be so offensive to others that they won't come near us, but true beauty radiates from a pure soul.

We all have intrinsic dignity; we are all valued and worthy of Heaven in God's eyes. Human bodies are not for human lust, pride, vanity, or any number of other sins. If these are the things our bodies were not created for, then who are we? What are we made for? We are made for the Glory of God; our highest calling is unity with our Creator.

Consider

Do you feel like your heart is pure? Are you internally motivated by a desire for Heaven? What connections can you draw from how you feel inside to how you look or want to look outside? Does your appearance need to change to better align with whom your heart belongs to? Does your heart need to change to reflect whose you are? How have the "no-make-up" days affected you? Have you skipped over them? Have you embraced them? You are beautiful!

PURITY & MODESTY: DAY 44

Our pursuit of holiness, of Heaven, begins in the heart. Our soul is sustained by the Holy Spirit, but our practice of the virtues will help our heart to be purified.

"Those whose hearts are pure are the temples of the Holy Spirit." – *St. Lucy*

For wisdom is a kindly spirit, yet she does not acquit blasphemous lips; Because God is the witness of the inmost self and the sure observer of the heart and the listener to the tongue. – *Wisdom 1:6*

So turn from youthful desires and pursue righteousness, faith, love, and peace, along with those who call on the Lord with purity of heart. Avoid foolish and ignorant debates, for you know that they breed quarrels. A slave of the Lord should not quarrel, but should be gentle with everyone, able to teach, tolerant, correcting opponents with kindness. It may be that God will grant them repentance that leads to knowledge of the truth, and that they may return to their senses out of the devil's snare, where they are entrapped by him, for his will. – *2 Timothy 2:22-26*

St. Lucy lived around the turn of the 4th century. She asked her mother to give away their money to the poor as Christ instructed, but her mother wanted to wait until closer to her death. She told her mother the pure thing to do is give now, be kind now, not wait for a "better" time. Although all of the details of her life aren't fully known, we do know that St. Lucy died a martyr when she wouldn't offer sacrifice to pagan gods, after having her eyes gouged out.

Like St. Lucy is quoted as saying, when our hearts are pure, we can be temples of the Holy Spirit, which ushers us to transcendent happiness. Letting the Holy Spirit make our hearts pure, we can't help but magnify the Lord. The Holy Spirit is the Love *flowing* between the Father and the Son. Modesty in the soul can be described as having a pure heart, pursing God's perfect love and peace while avoiding all the fleshy attachments.

2 Timothy has gentleness, teaching, correcting, and tolerance in the same instruction. In our time of so many competing "voices", we might feel like those actions and traits can't go together. We might believe that we should let others have their own "truth" out of a sense of fairness to their individuality (and, "Who are we to judge?"). But if we believe the Truth exists, it is unjust to let various false "truths" float around without at least praying to see if God is asking us to witness in word and deed. We are our brothers' and sisters' keepers. Virtue can't be practiced in a vacuum. The point of virtue is to help us live in right relationship. That is to say, proper unity with God and others.

Multiple truths make the very word "truth" irrelevant. Two differing thoughts about the same concrete thing cannot both simultaneously be true. Perhaps God wants us to be the one to blatantly speak out to someone in our life about Truth, but He may also not will us to be that person. That's why being docile to the Holy Spirit is important, yet again tying together the virtues.

Tolerance doesn't mean we let people go astray in the name of acceptance. Charity is loving people so much we want them to go to Heaven! We seek to build friendships with others. Out of gentleness and love of the person, we are able to sow seeds of faith, but it is up to God to provoke hearts to repentance. This is modesty in the soul—humility, recognizing we don't save anyone. Purity of heart lets God be God.

Fighting with others, maliciously arguing with people who are erroneous, or posting disrespectful sentiments on social media does no one any good. It leads us to sin and it doesn't convert others. Conversion and repentance are born out of love. A pure heart allows us to see God as He really is—bigger than our concept of Him. The hope we have for eternal life is belief in the Truth that God works beyond our understanding to extend grace to others. There is always hope, and a pure heart reminds us that this is what we must share with others through authentic friendships and charitable interactions.

Consider

Have you ever been corrected for a wrong belief within the Catholic Church? How was it given to you and how did you receive it? Is there someone in your life that needs to receive the Truth? Are you cultivating kindness in correction rather than harsh argumentation? Are you cautious to always convey Truth, Goodness, and Love, through purity of heart? How do you avoid less-tangible sins against purity and modesty, such as gossip and calumny?

PURITY & MODESTY: DAY 45

Purity of our body is important to God, as we are made in His image, as His creation. St. Jacinta heard much about this from Our Lady at Fatima.

"The sins which cause the most souls to go to hell are the sins of the flesh. Fashions will much offend Our Lord. People who serve God should not follow the fashions. The Church has no fashions. Our Lord is always the same. The sins of the world are very great." – *Our Lady to St. Jacinta*

"To be pure in body means to be chaste, and to be pure in mind means not to commit sins; not to look at what one should not see, not to steal or lie, and always to speak the truth, even if it is hard." – *Our Lady to St. Jacinta*

May the eyes of [your] hearts be enlightened, that you may know what is the hope that belongs to his call, what are the riches of glory in his inheritance among the holy ones, and what is the surpassing greatness of his power for us who believe, in accord with the exercise of his great might, which he worked in Christ, raising him from the dead and seating him at his right hand in the heavens, far above every principality, authority, power, and dominion, and every name that is named not only in this age but also in the one to come. And he put all things beneath his feet and gave him as head over all things to the church, which is his body, the fullness of the one who fills all things in every way. – *Ephesians 1:18-23*

As we read in Matthew 5:8, those that are pure in heart will see God. Our bodies are gifts from our Creator so that we can come to know and love Him, to experience His Divine Presence through our senses and not just our intellect. When we let our senses seek to please ourselves outside of what God desires for us, we do not have a pure heart; we aren't seeking the good of others nor bringing glory to God. We can't magnify the Lord when we have disordered priorities or desires; they go against the Greatest Commandment. Magnify 90 is a great time to organize our desires in the right way.

Though we often use it to describe a soul's "location", the heart is of the body. Our identity within our heart isn't how we are recognized by the senses of others because it is concealed within our chest. We are recognized most often by our face, by our head. Christ is the head of the body of believers; people know we are Christian because we follow Christ. So rather than the secular sentiment of "follow your heart," perhaps we should focus more on following our head—that is to say, Jesus Christ. We also have a seal on our head that says we belong to Him through baptism. Do we allow our body to confirm that seal into visible truth? Are we worldly in our appearance through conforming to lust-inducing trends or are we honoring our dignity and that of others through modest appearance (which can still be uplifting)? How are we attached to bodily comfort, lust, and vanity?

Recalling what Our Lady of Fatima said to St. Jacinta, we accept that hell is real and that sins of the flesh drive more people there than any other. She also tells us that fashions are not something Christians should ultimately be concerned with. They wax and they wane, but God is always the same. A sense of style can be affirming to femininity if done in a rightly ordered way, but many of today's "fashions" have no room in a virtuous woman's closet. We must join our bodily senses to our soul's intentions. Because He is a God of mercy, we can seek forgiveness when we fall. We have hope of Heaven because we keep trying to purify our hearts!

Consider

What body-driven impurities are surfacing during this Magnify 90? Do you show that you are a child of God or do you show that you belong to the world? What are some ways you can reveal your Christianity through your actions and appearance? Include "Oh Mercy" by Stu Garrard, Matt Maher and Audrey Assad as a part of your prayer. Utilize confession and God's Infinite Mercy to renew yourself in Him.

PURITY & MODESTY: DAY 46

The soul that we care about isn't external; it is internal. Thus, our external dress and appearance should reflect our interior life.

Your adornment should not be an external one: braiding the hair, wearing gold jewelry, or dressing in fine clothes, but rather the hidden character of the heart, expressed in the imperishable beauty of a gentle and calm disposition, which is precious in the sight of God. – *1 Peter 3:3-4*

CCC 2521: Purity requires modesty, an integral part of temperance. Modesty protects the intimate center of the person. It means refusing to unveil what should remain hidden. It is ordered to chastity to whose sensitivity it bears witness. It guides how one looks at others and behaves toward them in conformity with the dignity of persons and their solidarity.

2522: Modesty protects the mystery of persons and their love. It encourages patience and moderation in loving relationships; it requires that the conditions for the definitive giving and commitment of man and woman to one another be fulfilled. Modesty is decency. It inspires one's choice of clothing. It keeps silence or reserve where there is evident risk of unhealthy curiosity. It is discreet.

The passage from 1 Peter may be difficult to accept because we do like to have nice hair, accessories, and clothes. The passage is not saying we can't have those things. It is saying that those can't be our priorities. They don't help us get to Heaven, but interestingly they could keep us from Heaven. They shouldn't be what we think about, where we focus our energy, or where we spend our money. The word "adornment" here was translated from the Greek "kosmos," which usually is rendered as "world." So, the "world" that we are most concerned with should be our interior life, the spiritual realm. The way our interior life flows outward matters so much more than simple exterior beauty. What we look like and what we wear should be directed by our love for God, our love for others. Each human has dignity and is worthy of not being led into temptation by a sister or brother, so this is why St. Peter's writing encourages women to remember the most important thing is a life of virtue and character of the heart.

Given that we know our soul is an eternal creation, we must clothe our body with more than just physical clothes. We try to live apart from the culture that defines women on her ability to look good in a dress, leggings, or gym capris. We wear clothes for functionality, simplicity, and are conscious of what we may be inviting to the minds of others. We can't clothe ourselves for Heaven and ignore the fact that we are our brothers' and sisters' keepers. The over-used argument that people just "shouldn't look if they're going to be tempted or jealous" misses the mark. In charity and justice, we try to help others get to Heaven, and being modest in our appearance is a part of that.

The Blessed Mother would never call anyone into an impure desire or thought by her way of being or dressing. We are called to imitate this in our desire to magnify the Lord. Certainly, we don't have to dress frumpily, but we do have to be modest. Beauty in fashion should be timeless and feminine detailing in clothing gives us the opportunity to express ourselves as daughters of the King of Heaven.

Consider

Would you feel modest in all your outfits/swimsuits in our Blessed Mother's presence? Have you ever spent more time getting ready for the day than in meditative prayer? How do you respect others' dignity through your own dignity? If you have children, how do you practice modesty with them? How do you choose your Sunday best? If you'd like to, add "Undivided" by Stu Garrard & Amanda Cook as part of your prayer.

PURITY & MODESTY: DAY 47

We need to focus on incorruptibility despite the efforts of the devil and his influence on our culture of sex and minimal belief in the true God.

For that which is corruptible must clothe itself with incorruptibility, and that which is mortal must clothe itself with immortality. And when this which is corruptible clothes itself with incorruptibility and this which is mortal clothes itself with immortality, then the word that is written shall come about: "Death is swallowed up in victory. Where, O death, is your victory? Where, O death, is your sting?"– *1 Corinthians 15:53-55*

"When a man loves a woman, he has to become worthy of her. The higher her virtue, the more noble her character, the more devoted she is to truth, justice, goodness, the more a man has to aspire to be worthy of her. The history of civilization could actually be written in terms of the level of its women."
– *Venerable Fulton Sheen*

St. Paul in 1 Corinthians tells us why we must clothe ourselves with incorruptibility and immortality: so that death will have no victory over us; so we will see God's face. That is called the Beatific Vision; it's Heaven! We know that our current bodies are imperfect; corruptible. They can lead us astray with many insatiable desires against purity of mind and body. We cannot serve two masters—it's either God or our senses. We'll always be searching for something other than God unless we are striving for virtue. Contending for purity of heart keeps us focused on God alone and working for eternal happiness—sainthood.

Most of us want to be liked by others and we want to be happy right now. Those desires are at odds with the truth of God's love and desire for eternal happiness for us. Unfortunately, people will always let us down—we can't always be liked. So our life can't revolve around making others like us. We can try to be happy, but until we are in the fullness of God in Heaven, we must know we won't fully be happy. So happiness is a long marathon of a goal, with eternity as the big picture realization.

Living the virtues and living a life full of grace through the Sacraments, these are ways to pursue the goal. Humans just get misguided by ignoring the soul's desires through living only for the body's desires. When we chase after corruptible and mortal pleasures, we miss what we really need to thirst for: God alone. As we pursue modesty and purity of heart, we can't let the world's standards define our lifestyle.

We are all surely aware of the deep pains pornography causes those affected by it, and the effects of that industry's "success" are widespread. Sexual exploitation and lustful attitudes and behaviors have spilled over into every aspect of secular lives. Women's opinions of themselves are especially influenced by this culture. In general, we struggle with depression, eating disorders, and anxiety because we feel that our identity and worth is in our sexuality and appearance. It's seemingly out of control, as more and more money goes toward expensive mega-gym memberships, Botox or other physical alterations, diet pills, revealing clothes to prove our hard work on our body, and meal plans / status eating.

Many prioritize their day around getting a workout in rather than praying. Watching scandalous shows, where the human body is idolized, fill the evenings so that people can escape into a fantasy world that distracts them from the Truth. We can't realize we are worthy of God's love when we don't even act like humans are worth respect and dignity. We've lost ourselves when we seek our value in a world that doesn't love us like God does. He sees our potential for goodness, whereas the culture seeks to use us for its own benefit.

This is why Ven. Fulton Sheen said that women must be noble, so that those around us are called to a higher way of life as well. We must start by valuing ourselves as daughters of God, as feminine geniuses. We have to believe that we ARE worthy of Jesus' sacrifice, of pure love, and of our call to sainthood. We must revolt against the way of a sexualized, comfort-seeking world. We have to stop trying to blend in and instead stand out in our practice of virtue.

How have you struggled with the effects of pornography and the bar that it sets for women's sexuality? How can you combat the devil's lies that truth, beauty and goodness are relative? Do you see any personal connection between the bar women set for those around them and the way society behaves? Have you missed watching any secular TV shows during the Magnify 90? Why?

PURITY & MODESTY: DAY 48

Our perception of modesty is heavily influenced by our peers, our media intake, and the entertainment we seek out. Put good in, get good out.

CCC 2524: The forms taken by modesty vary from one culture to another. Everywhere, however, modesty exists as an intuition of the spiritual dignity proper to man. It is born with the awakening consciousness of being a subject. Teaching modesty to children and adolescents means awakening in them respect for the human person.

"Neither charity nor modesty can subsist without great humility and internal mortification of self-will, self-humor, and curiosity. The connection of these virtues should much encourage the religious soul to practice them; one will lead to the other." – Order of St. Clare (Convent of Poor Clares Dublin. *The Rule of the Holy Virgin Saint Clare.* (1856) Browne & Nolan)

"Love God, serve God, everything is in that." – St. Clare (Léopold de Chérancé. *St. Clare of Assisi.* (1910) R. & T. Washbourne)

Purity is always the same, but secular modesty is mostly related to how people of the time and place view dignity of the person. What is considered "modest in dress" is often connected to the culture. The no bare elbows or ankles "rule" of two centuries ago isn't a part of "modesty" today. It used to be inappropriate to have even nominally profane words on ads, TV, or music, but now this is (sadly) not the case at all! Men used to always wear suits to Mass or the office, but again, this cultural norm has passed. Because our world is moving closer and closer to anti-religion and missing a baseline understanding of dignity, we can see how 10-year-old girls end up wearing crop tops with their mother's approval and then end up depressed when they're objectified and not treated as beloved.

These virtues acknowledge that we are not the highest power; we cover ourselves out of humility and respect for the Sacred and Divine. In his book *Three to Get Married*, Ven. Fulton Sheen discusses that we keep sacred things "secret" (that is, veiled) not because we are afraid or want to hide them—but because we have reverence for them. We are in awe. Alice von Hildebrand also includes this topic in her book *Man and Woman: A Divine Invention* (2002, Sapientia Press Ave Maria Univ). The short summary of her take is that women would do well to realize their biological/physical ability to bring life into the world (whether than are actually able to or not aside), and the modesty it demands because they are "touched" by God in the sense of collaborating with Him in that most intimate gift.

If we accept that we are called to be holy—set-apart—our day-to-day lives must look different from someone who likes watching trashy TV and movies with sexual scenes. We make fashion choices that convey human dignity rather than sexual appetites. We welcome neighbors in for family-style dinners rather than hit up the club scene. By living a virtuous life, we can call attention to the reason for our joy: God! Befriending those that are struggling with purity can help us evangelize and give others a place from which to grow in mentorships, but we never buckle under the pressure to assimilate. Being set apart means just that: not blending into the culture. Perhaps we stand out by dressing up for mass, but being pure of heart calls us to remember reverence and love for God matters more than fitting in.

We are more likely to fall into sin when we are distracted by things of the flesh, including drinking, gluttony, media and sports intake, and gossip. Like St. Clare wrote above...let us be humble and fight against our selfish desires so that purity becomes one of our virtues!

Would a sinless woman watch this / listen to this / wear this / do this? If the answer is "no", DON'T do it. It is tempting to justify behaviors and desires because we are "only human," but you aren't made for settling. You are made to be a saint! Where in your journey have you seen love lead to purity, and/or purity lead to love? If purity and modesty are already in your wheelhouse, how are you encouraging your children or friends?

PURITY & MODESTY: DAY 49

The only valuable opinion is from God and He says you are loved, you can trust Him, and you can be pure of heart. Heaven is what you are made for. Live your life internally and externally to be a saint.

So submit yourselves to God. Resist the devil, and he will flee from you. Draw near to God, and he will draw near to you. Cleanse your hands, you sinners, and purify your hearts, you of two minds. – *James 4:7-8*

And if your right hand causes you to sin, cut it off and throw it away. It is better for you to lose one of your members than to have your whole body go into Gehenna. – *Matthew 5:30*

We cause no one to stumble in anything, in order that no fault may be found with our ministry; on the contrary, in everything we commend ourselves as ministers of God, through much endurance, in afflictions, hardships, constraints, beatings, imprisonments, riots, labors, vigils, fasts; by purity, knowledge, patience, kindness, in a holy spirit, in unfeigned love, in truthful speech, in the power of God; with weapons of righteousness at the right and at the left; through glory and dishonor, insult and praise. We are treated as deceivers and yet are truthful; as unrecognized and yet acknowledged; as dying and behold we live; as chastised and yet not put to death; as sorrowful yet always rejoicing; as poor yet enriching many; as having nothing and yet possessing all things. – *2 Corinthians 6:3-10*

We should always strive for Heaven. We should seek the Lord with such abandon that there's no room for the devil to work. Purgatory is not the goal, and if it is, we need to realize the suffering of purgatory is knowing how great God is and how far we still are from His fullness. Do we need to change our lifestyles to reflect where our heart is longing? Cut the sin off and throw it away, sisters! There's no middle ground when it comes to purity because if we give the devil an inch, he will come grab a mile. We must let God purify our faith, hearts, and bodily desires through our own pursuit of virtue. As St. Therese says, "You cannot be half a saint, you must be a whole saint or no saint at all."(letter to Abbe Maurice Belliere, June 21, 1897)

To resist the devil takes power out of his hands and aids our virtuous growth. If we can't resist the devil with respect to purity right now, change is necessary. We need to stop listening to that voice which tells us we need to look a certain way to be valued, or that we need to have a certain thing to be worthy. We are worthy of God's love and we are valued by Him just by our very creation. Can we stop being *attached* to being appreciated or found worthy by other humans? This is called the sin of human acceptance. It falls under pride, but it's also affected by vices against purity and modesty. Perhaps one of the most challenging pieces of Magnify 90 is praying the Litany of Humility daily and really, *truly* meaning it. This will be a lifelong journey, so we pray that the Lord will purify our intentions for magnifying Him and give us the strength to reach that goal.

Consider

"You might be the only gospel that anyone ever reads." Take the Scripture verses to heart today. Pray with them, journal, meditate on how they relate to your current struggles. What attachments have you seen during this Magnify 90: how can you "cut it off" so that the last half is freer? How can joy really take over your soul? Who or what is truly ruling your life? If you'd like, include "King of My Heart" by John Mark & Sarah McMillan as a part of your prayer.

WEEKLY REFLECTIONS

Prayerfulness

St. Faustina &
Mother Angelica

WEEK 8 - PRAYERFULNESS
St. Faustina & Mother Angelica

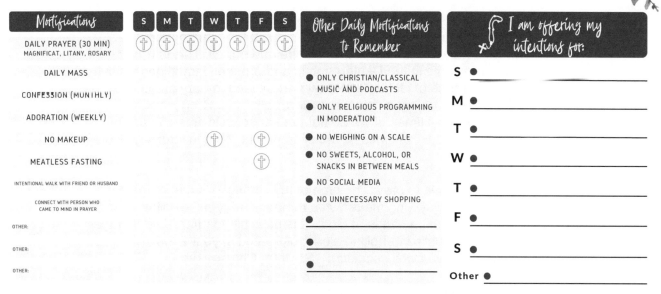

Mortifications	S	M	T	W	T	F	S
DAILY PRAYER (30 MIN) MAGNIFICAT, LITANY, ROSARY	✝	✝	✝	✝	✝	✝	✝
DAILY MASS							
CONFESSION (MONTHLY)							
ADORATION (WEEKLY)							
NO MAKEUP			✝			✝	
MEATLESS FASTING						✝	
INTENTIONAL WALK WITH FRIEND OR HUSBAND							
CONNECT WITH PERSON WHO CAME TO MIND IN PRAYER							
OTHER:							
OTHER:							
OTHER:							

Other Daily Mortifications to Remember

- ONLY CHRISTIAN/CLASSICAL MUSIC AND PODCASTS
- ONLY RELIGIOUS PROGRAMMING IN MODERATION
- NO WEIGHING ON A SCALE
- NO SWEETS, ALCOHOL, OR SNACKS IN BETWEEN MEALS
- NO SOCIAL MEDIA
- NO UNNECESSARY SHOPPING
- _____
- _____
- _____

I am offering my intentions for:

- S _____
- M _____
- T _____
- W _____
- T _____
- F _____
- S _____
- Other _____

Express Use this space to journal, draw, or otherwise express your thoughts on this week's virtue. Spend some time listening to the Holy Spirit, perhaps in Adoration, and capture whatever He brings to mind or lays on your heart.

PRAYERFULNESS: DAY 50

This week we focus on prayerfulness as a virtue and our invitation as Christians to *pray without ceasing*.

CCC 2697: Prayer is the life of the new heart. It ought to animate us at every moment. But we tend to forget him who is our life and our all. This is why the Fathers of the spiritual life in the Deuteronomic and prophetic traditions insist that prayer is a remembrance of God often awakened by the memory of the heart "We must remember God more often than we draw breath." (St. Gregory of Nazianzus) But we cannot pray "at all times" if we do not pray at specific times, consciously willing it These are the special times of Christian prayer, both in intensity and duration.

2743: It is always possible to pray: The time of the Christian is that of the risen Christ who is with us always, no matter what tempests may arise. (Matthew 28:20; Luke 8:24) Our time is in the hands of God: "It is possible to offer fervent prayer even while walking in public or strolling alone, or seated in your shop,… while buying or selling,…or even while cooking." (St. John Chrysostom)

2744: Prayer is a vital necessity. Proof from the contrary is no less convincing: if we do not allow the Spirit to lead us, we fall back into the slavery of sin. (Galatians 5:16-25) How can the Holy Spirit be our life if our heart is far from him? […]

Prayer is not *optional* in the Christian life. As the Catechism says, *praying at all times* is not the same as *saying prayers* at all times. Praying at all times often looks like inviting God into our life in the present moment. It can be rote, memorized prayers; reading scripture and meditating upon it; or it may be singing praise songs, chanting psalms. But most devotedly, it's keeping a conversation with God going all throughout the day. When we go for a run, when we go to the store, when we speak with friends or family (or even those who irritate us), when we work on the computer or on the job site, or when we dine out or cook a meal, everything we do can be offered to God for His glory as we seek to magnify Him. Every moment of every day is an opportunity to be loved and to share love. Love is a prayer. Practicing virtue is a prayer and so is recognizing our shortcomings when we offer them back to God.

God wants us to be in relationship with Him, to consider Him both Father and friend above all friends. Our 90 days of growing in virtue, so that we can magnify Him, can only work if we pray; otherwise we may find ourselves easily slipping into pride for a box checked off on achieving a life of mortification rather than an offering of devotion and desire for holiness in detachment.

God is always faithful and those that stay in contact with Him can recognize His loving presence amidst the challenges. When we stay rooted in conversation with God, we can better identify our sins and failings; we can flee from vice and pursue virtue by trying to share His loving goodness with others.

Lord Jesus, Humble Ruler, you came down to the world and taught us by word and example how to pray and the importance of praying often. We are grateful for your patient guidance and ask that you continue to pour your grace into our lives. We humbly invite your Holy Spirit to guide us at all times that we may increasingly fulfill Your Most Holy Will. Amen.

Have you tried to deepen your prayer life through Magnify 90? Has offering up mortifications for others made self-denial feel like a prayer? Can you approach a challenging situation better by praying in your mind while dealing with it? Identify one mundane part of your day-to-day life today during which to have a conversation with God.

PRAYERFULNESS: DAY 51

Although we don't want prayer to simply be a box we check off, we do have to cultivate the habit of asking God what He thinks about any given situation. "He must increase; I must decrease." (John 3:30)

CCC 2725: Prayer is both a gift of grace and a determined response on our part. It always presupposes effort. The great figures of prayer of the Old Covenant before Christ, as well as the Mother of God, the saints, and he himself, all teach us this: prayer is a battle. Against whom? Against ourselves and against the wiles of the tempter who does all he can to turn man away from prayer, away from union with God. We pray as we live, because we live as we pray. If we do not want to act habitually according to the Spirit of Christ, neither can we pray habitually in his name. The "spiritual battle" of the Christian's new life is inseparable from the battle of prayer.

"The object of our prayer-life is to empty ourselves and be filled with the Trinity." – *Mother Angelica* (Mother Angelica. *Mother Angelica on Suffering and Burnout.* (2017) EWTN Publishing)

The very ability to pray is a gift from God, a grace. But as with any grace, we have to *receive* the gift and open it; we have to do something with the gift. Prayer can often feel impossible because we have to seek a relationship with the Creator of the world, who is bigger than our concept of time and space. The devil will tempt us to think we don't have time to pray, we don't need to pray, or maybe the devil might even try to convince us that we can't pray because of our sins, our doubts, or our secret deep self-loathing. We must recognize this and stop it in its tracks! Our only fair response to the "invitation to unity with God" is forming the habit of prayer.

If we want to live a life on earth that leads to an eternity of happiness, we must pray through the busyness, we must pray when we have nothing to say, and we must certainly pray even when we've sinned, doubted, and been ashamed. If we can't find the words to say, reading Psalm 139 is a good place to start, or the Lord's Prayer, or simply repeating *Jesus, I trust in you*! Just showing up is often the hardest part.

God won't be reflected by our lives if we are full of ourselves and our own interests. During our 90 days in this "desert," we've been trying to get rid of our vices, so we are then able to live a life in the Spirit. We know full well that it is easy to become weary and maybe even give up on our prayer life if we aren't pursuing virtue intentionally. And the minute we think we've got it all figured out, we need to pray for God to reveal the places we are ignoring our need for growth.

Come Holy Spirit and fill what we have emptied, ready and waiting to be filled by you. May we never forget God's life-giving faithfulness, lest we fall into the life-draining temptations of the world. May we go out renewed, refreshed, and filled with love to serve God in the places He is calling us. Amen.

Consider

Detachment can be a lengthy, painful process. What are you still struggling with at this point in Magnify 90? Why do you think that is? Take your attachments to prayer and sincerely ask God to help you detach. If you don't want to do that, pray that you may want to pray that prayer. Consider spending some time prayerfully reflecting on "Rest in God Alone" by Adam Bitter.

PRAYERFULNESS: DAY 52

There's an ironic experience that being in the desert to rid ourselves of temptations opens us up to new temptations of despair or scrupulosity. Jesus experienced spiritual attacks from the devil in the desert as well, so we can feel consolation in walking in His footsteps.

Rejoice in hope, endure in affliction, persevere in prayer. – *Romans 12:12*

CCC 1817: Hope is the theological virtue by which we desire the kingdom of heaven and eternal life as our happiness, placing our trust in Christ's promises and relying not on our own strength, but on the help of the grace of the Holy Spirit [...]

1821: We can therefore hope in the glory of heaven promised by God to those who love him and do his will. (Romans 8:28) In every circumstance, each one of us should hope, with the grace of God, to persevere "to the end" (Matthew 20:22) and to obtain the joy of heaven, as God's eternal reward for the good works accomplished with the grace of Christ. In hope, the Church prays for "all men to be saved." (1 Timothy 2:4) She longs to be united with Christ, her Bridegroom, in the glory of heaven: *Hope, O my soul, hope. You know neither the day nor the hour. Watch carefully, for everything passes quickly, even though your impatience makes doubtful what is certain, and turns a very short time into a long one. Dream that the more you struggle, the more you prove the love that you bear your God, and the more you will rejoice one day with your Beloved, in a happiness and rapture that can never end. (St. Teresa of Avila)*

Perhaps we've previously experienced a beautiful connection with God, a taste of transcendent happiness. But because we are still open to the devil's temptations while on earth, we have feelings that convince us we are isolated and maybe we are even depressed. However close we once felt like we had drawn to the Lord, the farther we may feel at other times. We may cry sorrowful tears and think we will never feel His loving embrace again. Our feelings can often lead us into despair; feelings are often the devil's playground. We must cling to the *Truth* that has been revealed and even detach from our emotions.

We *know* we receive graces; yet, God permits us to feel tempted amongst the trials of this life. Our taste of transcendent happiness is missing for (long) periods of time. Seeking that deep connection with God again, we visit the adoration chapel, go to confession and receive the Blessed Sacrament at Mass, sing a praise song, or read encouraging scripture. Nothing changes in our emotions. When we've done "all" the personal and internal things, we can seek communion with God; we need to remember that He is also found outside ourselves and our expectations—in others and in Truth and in *being* (not doing). We need to love God for Who He is and yearn for His peace in our souls that we can often only find in prayer and service to others.

Despite our human emotions, dryness *should* encourage us to persevere in prayerfulness because even our attachment to feelings will get in the way of our truest desire to be a saint. Do we like the *feeling* of union with God?

Of course, but should that be why we pray? Even the greatest saints have felt a loneliness in prayer that is described as "dryness"—because it seems the Living Water is far from them, like in a desert. This is where the theological virtue of hope comes in. We can have communion with God regardless of dryness.

Prayer as the watering can to our soul's thirst for God opens our eyes to mercy and love. Prayer *is* hope. We hope that the Lord will grant us eternal life because we trust in His mercy. We hope that by thirsting for His righteousness, we will become saints. The desert is the perfect place to pray for hope, in hope.

Dear Lord, thank you for the gift of the faithful who have lived before us and modeled what it is to persevere in prayer. Give us the strength to overcome any temptation not to pray and to never weary in the battle to grow closer to you. Amen. St. Michael, pray for us!

Consider: How do you identify spiritual attacks? What are the hallmarks of an attack by the devil on your particular soul? How can you make the time to pray even when it feels tedious or impossible? Today, keep God always present through your senses—light a candle when you pray, listen to chant or praise, grasp a rosary or palm cross, use holy water, receive the Eucharist if you can. How does filling your senses on faith-filled things affect your feelings? For further meditation, read 2 Corinthians 1:1-11 and CCC 1820.

PRAYERFULNESS: DAY 53

We may be tempted to avoid dedicated prayer time if we don't feel we can do it properly. That's the devil speaking. Prayer must be all encompassing of our lives; God wants our whole heart, not just a blessing before meals.

CCC 2729: The habitual difficulty in prayer is distraction. It can affect words and their meaning in vocal prayer; it can concern, more profoundly, him to whom we are praying, in vocal prayer (liturgical or personal), meditation, and contemplative prayer. To set about hunting down distractions would be to fall into their trap, when all that is necessary is to turn back to our heart: for a distraction reveals to us what we are attached to, and this humble awareness before the Lord should awaken our preferential love for him and lead us resolutely to offer him our heart to be purified. Therein lies the battle, the choice of which master to serve (see Matthew 6: 21, 24).

Purposely to allow one's mind to wander in prayer is sinful and hinders the prayer from having fruit. It is against this that [St.] Augustine says in his Rule: *"When you pray God with psalms and hymns, let your mind attend to that which your lips pronounce."* But to wander in mind unintentionally does not deprive prayer of its fruit. Hence [St.] Basil says *"If you are so truly weakened by sin that you are unable to pray attentively, strive as much as you can to curb yourself, and God will pardon you, seeing that you are unable to stand in His presence in a becoming manner, not through negligence but through frailty."* – *St. Thomas Aquinas, Summa Theologiae II-II, Q83 a13r3*

"You see, I must be at home with God; then my whole life becomes a prayer. I cannot speak with God if I have not "lived" a prayer all day! ... You cannot rush in from the world and be filled with its concerns." – *Mother Angelica (Mother Angelica. Little Book of Life Lessons and Everyday Spirituality* (2007) Doubleday)

Our pursuit of prayerfulness as a virtue will be substantially, even infinitely, harder without striving to remove sin from our lives. We need humility to pray as we ought, because *He is God*, we are not. It is truly necessary that we go about our daily lives, caring for our family or apostolate, giving our body its basic needs, working as God intended us to participate in His creation. But prayerfulness looks like intentionally taking time for silence and attention to God alone. We can't just pray a 20 second bedtime prayer and think our relationship with our Creator will thrive.

Prayerfulness is a virtue within justice because it is *only* fair to listen to and silently focus on He who made us. It takes faith to let our mind focus only on God because that means we are surrendering control—of all the other things we have been thinking about—to Him. Things we are distracted by should pass through our mind onto the Lord and we should be released from obsession or anxiety.

Are we attached to our tasks at work/home? Or to our children's schedules? Our own hunger or tiredness? If we have already offered these to the Lord as we experience or plan them, then our prayer time can be calmly intentional. When thoughts do distract us from silently abiding in the Lord, let us offer them as petitions, then quickly move back into the realm of adoring God simply for Who He is. Not only can our whole life be a prayer, but distractions from intimacy with the Lord should become part of our intentions.

Merciful God, forgive us when we are distracted by earthly burdens during our time with You. Give us the grace to hand over all concerns to You so that we may be free from anxiety and worry. In doing so, may we more easily determine Your Will and have the courage to heed your guidance. Amen.

What things do you most often find your mind drifting towards in prayer? How does this reveal attachment? When has your soul felt most peaceful? Make one personal resolution today to increase the intentionality and attentiveness of your dedicated prayer time, be it duration, location or renewing your commitment to daily prayer.

PRAYERFULNESS: DAY 54

There are a lot of voices to listen to but harken only to the Good Shepherd's voice: "My sheep hear my voice; I know them, and they follow me." (John 10:27) Reflect on excerpts from St. Faustina's diary regarding prayer, pursuing silence in contemplation.

"When you reflect upon what I tell you in the depths of your heart, you profit more than if you had read many books. Oh, if souls would only want to listen to My voice when I am speaking in the depths of their hearts, they would reach the peak of holiness in a short time." *(No. 584, Diary of Saint Maria Faustina Kowalska (1987) Marian Fathers)*

"The Holy Spirit does not speak to a soul that is distracted and garrulous (meaning talkative). He speaks by His quiet inspirations to a soul that is recollected, to a soul that knows how to keep silence." *(No. 552, Diary of Saint Maria Faustina Kowalska (1987) Marian Fathers)*

My soul, be at rest in God alone, from whom comes my hope. God alone is my rock and my salvation, my fortress; I shall not fall. – *Psalm 62:6-7*

Prayerfulness is pondering, which is to "think about something carefully, especially before making a decision or reaching a conclusion." The Greek word used in reference to Mary's pondering (see Luke 2) is *sumballó*, which literally means "putting together"; so too are we called to make God's will our own through putting it together.

How tempting it is to feel pride in our prayer life when we complete a checklist of prayers or holy readings, but Jesus wants us to listen to His voice out of free love not strict servitude. This is why working toward contemplative prayer is so significant! Simply letting the Holy Spirit flood our souls is vital to growing closer to God. To magnify the Lord, we must know the Lord, and to know Him, we must be quiet and listen. Then, only then, should we resolve to do something out of docility.

Often, we are scared of silence. Listening to God in silence hurts when we are afraid. Maybe we are worried of what God may place on our hearts. Maybe we feel nervous in the silence; we feel exposed, our bare souls laid out for what they really are: weak and needy. We often cringe at the thought of being described as "needy." But how true this is! We are truly needy. We *need* Jesus. We don't need a glass of wine. We don't need a snack or a nap. We don't need a TV show to "unwind." What we need, what we really thirst for, is the Truth that we are made for more, and there shall we live, abiding with Christ in our soul.

Be not afraid, sisters! Spend time in recollection, ready and willing to accept God's call — knowing that is the way to holiness. All the virtues will be fortified in our spirit of true prayerfulness. And virtue leads to sainthood, as it did for our Blessed Mother Mary, true exemplar of prayerful contemplation.

Come Holy Spirit, fill our hearts and minds with your quiet inspirations. Give us the grace to accept Your Will and the courage to act upon it. May we realize the path to holiness is not paved by our will, but Yours. Jesus, I trust in You!

When have you experienced pure joy of the soul? Was it when you *did* something or when you received something? What is your experience with contemplative prayer? Do you struggle with silence? Do you actually *want* to listen to His voice? What if you feel called to do or say something the culture looks at as *different*? If you'd like, add "The Father's House" by Cory Asbury as part of your prayer today.

PRAYERFULNESS: DAY 55

Prayer is obviously necessary in life's hard details, but it is in the routine of life that we must think of prayerfulness as a virtue with three expressions: vocal, meditation, and contemplation. See CCC 2700- 2724.

"Suffering is a great grace; through suffering the soul becomes like the Savior; in suffering love becomes crystallized; the greater the suffering, the purer the love." *(No. 57, Diary of Saint Maria Faustina Kowalska (1987) Marian Fathers)*

Then Jesus said to his disciples, "Whoever wishes to come after me must deny himself, take up his cross, and follow me." – *Matthew 16:24*

CCC 2716: Contemplative prayer is hearing the Word of God. Far from being passive, such attentiveness is the obedience of faith, the unconditional acceptance of a servant, and the loving commitment of a child. It participates in the "Yes" of the Son become servant and the Fiat of God's lowly handmaid.

When life is chugging along "fine," we can slip into a passive approach to prayer. We may simply read a meditation and make no resolution; we may speak some vocal prayers without really pausing to reflect on their meaning, then go back to our regular comfort-seeking lives. Then we get overwhelmed with situations, disappointed with the way people treat us, or anxious about choices to make. We hand our brain space over to other things, find some coping tools, and before we know it, fall out of the habit of daily prayer. But to stop the cycle, we must bring our cares before the Lord, even when we just want to wallow in self-pity or scroll through distractions on our phones. He wants us to rely on Him. We have to get over ourselves! We have to open our hearts and go deeper into our interior prayer life with the lover of our souls. Cultivating a habit of prayer isn't checking off a box; it's developing a relationship, even though we may need to hold ourselves accountable through writing down our plans to tangibly feel committed to our prayer life. Sainthood demands a relationship with God, not just knowledge about Him.

Our crosses, voluntary or involuntary, are the pathway to that relationship, because that is the model Jesus left us. We pick them up and follow him through hardship—cancer, death of a loved one, miscarriage, infertility, or infant loss, developing a physical or mental disability ourselves, or caring for someone with special needs. These are hard experiences that can lead us deeper into prayer, because we lean into relationship with God for strength. Prayer keeps us from losing faith in God who unites us to His Heart, even in pain. Prayer is an act of faith. The deepest prayer we can offer is acceptance that physical healing may never take place, so we let our suffering be transformed into an offering of unity with Christ.

When the "big" sufferings like those aren't really a part of our day-to-day, that is the time to deny our pleasure- or power-seeking behaviors, so that we can truly sense the Lord's will in our lives. During Magnify 90 we offer our sacrifices for a specific intention each day; it makes it much more meaningful to go without a comfort when it's a prayerful choice. We are called to self-giving love, to care about others' salvation as well as our own. We find His mystery, His salvific mission.

Lord Jesus Christ, Prince of Peace, we thank you for your faithfulness even in the times when we forget to pray and pause to honor your goodness. Be with us always and give us the grace to pray like You did to Your heavenly father—not my will, but Yours. Fill us with a peace the world cannot give. Amen.

In what situation(s) in these 55 days have you neglected to pray; have you tried to do it on your own? Have a spiritual sister keep you accountable! Before bed tonight, think of 3 things you are grateful for, 2 things you are sorry for, and 1 thing you resolve to do tomorrow.

PRAYERFULNESS: DAY 56

Mary shows us how to pray as we desire to magnify the Lord; we are called to be daughter, mother, spouse as she is.

And Mary said: "My soul proclaims the greatness of the Lord; my spirit rejoices in God my savior." – *Luke 1:46-47*

CCC 965: After her Son's Ascension, Mary "aided the beginnings of the Church by her prayers." (Lumen Gentium 69) In her association with the apostles and several women, "we also see Mary by her prayers imploring the gift of the Spirit, who had already overshadowed her in the Annunciation." (LG 59)

"I must strive to make the interior of my soul a resting place for the Heart of Jesus." *(No. 275, Diary of Saint Maria Faustina Kowalska (1987)* Marian Fathers*)*

"I want to be completely transformed into Your mercy and to be Your living reflection, O Lord." *(No. 163, Diary of Saint Maria Faustina Kowalska (1987)* Marian Fathers*)*

Mary lived her life praying at all times—her connection to God has never ceased aiding the church. In a uniquely perfect way she was daughter of the Father, Mother of the Son, and spouse of the Holy Spirit. While we aren't living our lives free of sin like Mary, we have hope for living out a feminine genius spirituality that is receptive, generous, sensitive, and maternal. God delights in us!

We make our souls inviting to Jesus through our prayer and practice of virtue. Our fallen nature is not an excuse to let sin consume us; we are asked to overcome this concupiscence most especially by prayerfulness. This further leads us to detachment and a sense of transformation. Prayer *is* transformational. It is only through prayer that we can even begin to have exterior lives of goodness. This requires seeking union with the Holy Spirit who alone teaches us to pray. Mary's example to magnify the Lord is our goal in prayer.

Magnify 90 can't just be a "program" of virtue growth alone, nor can it be one of solely penitential practices. Both pieces are needed because if we are emptying something, we must fill it back up with something other than sinful pride. If we are pursuing virtue, it won't stick if we aren't free of attachments, nor rooted in prayer. How quickly we can spiral from virtue to vice when we let ourselves get comfortable and lukewarm in prayer.

Come Holy Spirit, living in Mary, make our hearts pure and holy like hers. Thank you for giving us the example of our Mother Mary as what we should strive for in prayer—proclaiming the Lord's greatness at all times. May we reflect and ponder on Your faithfulness throughout the day—never losing our connection to You. Amen.

Consider

What do we learn in prayer? What do we say to God? What do we hear from Him? What do we see in prayer? Do we provide a place for Jesus to dwell, like Mary did? Do we comfort the wounds of Jesus like Mary did? Do we show others mercy, rather than seeking to fill our own needs first? When we encounter another person, do we provide a listening ear and an affirmation of love in Truth?

Now ponder some tangible ways you are being called to proclaim and rejoice in the Lord amongst today's society. What kind of a difference does your disposition make in your sphere of influence? Actions are empty if interior prayerfulness is lacking. Use the space below or a separate journal to reflect on today's theme and reflection. Recommit to daily prayer as needed.

WEEKLY REFLECTIONS

Zeal

St. Catherine of Siena

WEEK 9 - ZEAL
St. Catherine of Siena

Mortifications	S	M	T	W	T	F	S
DAILY PRAYER (30 MIN) MAGNIFICAT, LITANY, ROSARY	✝	✝	✝	✝	✝	✝	✝
DAILY MASS							
CONFESSION (MONTHLY)							
ADORATION (WEEKLY)							
NO MAKEUP		✝				✝	
MEATLESS FASTING						✝	
INTENTIONAL WALK WITH FRIEND OR HUSBAND							
CONNECT WITH PERSON WHO CAME TO MIND IN PRAYER							
OTHER:							
OTHER:							
OTHER:							

Other Daily Mortifications to Remember

- ● ONLY CHRISTIAN/CLASSICAL MUSIC AND PODCASTS
- ● ONLY RELIGIOUS PROGRAMMING IN MODERATION
- ● NO WEIGHING ON A SCALE
- ● NO SWEETS, ALCOHOL, OR SNACKS IN BETWEEN MEALS
- ● NO SOCIAL MEDIA
- ● NO UNNECESSARY SHOPPING
- ● _____
- ● _____
- ● _____

I am offering my intentions for:

- S ● _____
- M ● _____
- T ● _____
- W ● _____
- T ● _____
- F ● _____
- S ● _____
- Other ● _____

Express Use this space to journal, draw, or otherwise express your thoughts on this week's virtue. Spend some time listening to the Holy Spirit, perhaps in Adoration, and capture whatever He brings to mind or lays on your heart.

ZEAL: DAY 57

Zeal carries this idea of boldness, of a sort of power. Though power can have many meanings, we reflect on it meaning our ability to know truth and do good. Can we live out love in action when we are just showing up to check off a box?

For God did not give us a spirit of cowardice but rather of power and love and self-control. So do not be ashamed of your testimony to our Lord… but bear your share of hardship for the gospel with the strength that comes from God. He saved us and called us to a holy life, not according to our works but according to his own design and the grace bestowed on us in Christ Jesus before time began, but now made manifest through the appearance of our savior Christ Jesus, who destroyed death and brought life and immortality to light through the gospel… – *2 Timothy 1:7-11*

I wanted to show you that I am not much pleased with one who simply shouts, "Lord, Lord, I would like to do something for you!" nor with one who wishes to kill the body with great penances without slaying the selfish will. What I want is many works of patient and courageous endurance and of the other virtues I have described to you--interior virtues that are all active in bearing the fruit of grace. ... I want works of penance and other bodily practice to be undertaken as means, not as your chief goal. [...] But the merit of penance rests completely in the power of charity enlightened by true discernment. (St. Catherine of Siena. *The Dialogue* (1980) Paulist Press)

"Thus the devil neither is nor shall be routed by the suffering of our bodies, but by strength of the fire of divine, most ardent, and immeasurable love." – St. Catherine (St. Catherine of Siena. *St. Catherine of Siena as Seen in Her Letters* (1905) EP Dutton & Co)

What kind of power is St. Paul talking about in his letter to St. Timothy? The English "power" in this verse is translated from the Greek *dunamis*, which means "ability to perform," which is potential, effectiveness, possibility. God gives us the ability, the option, to grow in sanctification. We have this great potential, this great capacity, for holiness. We are capable of sainthood and living out zeal for bringing Him glory in all we do. God created us in His image, but we can deny it by not exercising that power—He desires we freely choose Him. Our free "yes" is shown in our loving self-sacrifice and choosing virtue.

Holiness hinges on enflaming our hearts for God's will, even our ability to prayerfully handle involuntary sufferings. Connected with what God reveals through St. Catherine, He doesn't make us saints just because we take up our crosses; we are made saints when we fully accept His love and mercy. To give up snacking for a few months doesn't change us if we don't first acknowledge that being in God's presence is ultimately better than eating. We must grow our love and devotion, or else we will just go right back to disordered attachments. Being able to avoid wine, have a naked face, or not watch TV isn't because we are powerful or strong. It is because *our love is for more.*

Suffering does not beat the devil, only Love does. Penance is pointless if we do it just to say we did it, or worse, to prove something! When things get hard, whether spiritually or physically, we have a choice. When we rely on Him, rather than ourselves, we assent to the Truth that true freedom pursues goodness, not just running away from something bad. The power given from the Holy Spirit is so we can desire Heaven out of love, not fear. Penances and trials of this life are permitted by God not to help us overcome evil, but rather so we can grow in love of God even when it isn't easy through our free will.

Consider the things you said you couldn't commit to at the beginning of Magnify 90. If you've grown in prayer and virtue over the past 8 weeks, are you now able to deny yourself a comfort that isn't really necessary? Alternately, are you attached to becoming detached? How does that relate to the need for docility to balance zeal? Is being prideful even in penance a struggle for you?

ZEAL: DAY 58

Zeal is virtuous when we want to advance the Kingdom of God, when we magnify Him to others for the sanctification of souls, and when we want to bring God glory in all we do.

CCC 828: By canonizing some of the faithful, i.e., by solemnly proclaiming that they practiced heroic virtue and lived in fidelity to God's grace, the Church recognizes the power of the Spirit of holiness within her and sustains the hope of believers by proposing the saints to them as models and intercessors. (Lumen Gentium 40; 48-51) "The saints have always been the source and origin of renewal in the most difficult moments in the Church's history." (St. John Paul II) Indeed, "holiness is the hidden source and infallible measure of her apostolic activity and missionary zeal." (Christifideles Laici 17, 3)

Go therefore and make disciples of all nations, baptizing them in the name of the Father and of the Son and of the Holy Spirit, teaching them to observe all that I have commanded you; and lo, I am with you always, to the close of the age.
– Matthew 19:18-20

And he said to him, "You shall love the Lord your God with all your heart, and with all your soul, and with all your mind. This is the great and first commandment. And a second is like it, you shall love your neighbor as yourself. *– Matthew 22:37-39*

Then she must love her neighbors with such affection that she would bear any pain or torment to win them the life of grace, ready to die a thousand deaths, if that were possible, for their salvation. And all her material possessions are at the service of her neighbors' physical needs. *(St. Catherine of Siena. The Dialogue (1980) Paulist Press)*

A truly zealous soul cannot be lukewarm. We can tell, in many ways, if we're growing tepid by how much we care about the salvation of others. Have we closed in on ourselves? Not only is that prideful, it's completely un-Christian. We are here on earth to care about others!

The Church exists to bring the Good News of salvation to the entire world. We can't truly pursue sainthood if we don't recognize that from our desire for salvation follows a desire for all souls' salvation. The desire we have for holiness must encourage holiness for others! We set about this desert of self-denial on one hand because we want to go to Heaven, and on the other hand because we want others to go to Heaven. Our pursuit of virtue should positively impact the way we live our lives and inspire those around us to grow closer to God as well.

It's uncharitable and simply not good to believe eternal life with God is the transcendent happiness yet not witness that truth to others through our zeal. We can't *give* other people faith, but sharing our own brokenness and longings can be opportunities to show God's mercy active in our life. This can beget hope for those around us. We may inspire others to be receptive to God when we walk the walk of a zealous yet imperfect and still trying Christian.

Zeal is vital to love. Jesus is Love in action; the saints were love in action; we are called to be love in action. Magnify 90 gives us a chance to grow closer to some amazing female saints, deepen our appreciation of scripture, and dive into the depth of wisdom in the *Catechism of the Catholic Church*. Let us utilize this knowledge to grow in our own virtue so that words of Truth become lives of Truth.

Has the zeal of someone in your life affected your faith? What difficulties do you face in being zealous? Can you make one resolution today to show love in action? How would those in your sphere of influence be affected if you fully lived out zeal without fear? If you struggle with being bold, is it because you fear judgement from others? Have you considered the sin of human respect (see below) in your examination of conscience before?

Since human respect is a kind of fear of the judgment of others, one acting from this motive lacks courage or fortitude, but as a vice human respect seems more directly opposed to magnanimity because it seeks honor rather than the works worthy of honor. [...] But the common human tendency to be concerned about the favorable opinion of others can be put to better use. If care is taken to associate with those who hold virtue in honor, the desire for the approval of others can encourage one to right living.
– *Dictionary of Moral Theology.*
(Compiled under the direction of Francesco Cardinal Roberti. Edited under the direction of Pietro Palazzini. Translated from the second Italian edition under the direction of Henry J. Yannone. (1962) Newman Press)

ZEAL: DAY 59

St. Catherine of Siena provides an amazing example of zeal. Her conversation with God in *The Dialogue* speaks at length about virtue and zeal for souls.

Virtue, once conceived, must come to birth. Therefore, as soon as the soul has conceived through loving affection, she gives birth for her neighbors' sake. And just as she loves me in truth, so also she serves her neighbors in truth. Nor could she do otherwise, for love of me and love of neighbor are one and the same thing: Since love of neighbor has its source in me, the more the soul loves me, the more she loves her neighbors. Such is the means I have given you to practice and prove your virtue. The service you cannot render me you must do for your neighbors. [...]

You see, in the face of their unfaithfulness and lack of hope you prove your own faith. And whenever it may be necessary to prove your virtue, you prove it both in yourself and through your neighbors... [...] And in the face of envy, spite, and hatred your loving charity is revealed in hungry desire for the salvation of souls. *(St. Catherine of Siena. The Dialogue (1980) Paulist Press)*

Despite being a woman living nearly 700 years ago, we know a lot about St. Catherine of Siena, in part because she had dedicated biographers in her confessor and friends, and because she inspired popes. But most specifically, because God set her apart as a role model for women who've come after her. As one of 4 female doctors of the church, she is well worth learning about as we strive to live out our own feminine genius. While we are each called to our own specific journey toward heaven, St. Catherine's life of detachment and zeal serves as a reminder that our lives must seek to be for God's glory alone, no matter our vocation.

St. Catherine lived a celibate life in the world, as a Dominican tertiary, which meant she wasn't a fully promised religious nun within the walls of a convent but wore the Dominican habit and didn't marry. St. Catherine traveled to spread the call to Christian renewal, repentance, and reliance on God out of total love and abandonment to His Providence. When they regarded her as crazy, St. Catherine would imagine her dismissive parents and others as Jesus, Mary, and the apostles. She sought to serve them in love as she would if it were Christ directly in front of her. Essentially, St. Catherine knew of God's love for her and felt love for Him, and flowing from that relationship was the desire for other souls to enter into communion with the Triune God as well.

Our desire to be women of virtue is not so difficult when we are surrounded by like-minded faithful Catholics, and, oh, how much we like being around people that "fill our cup"! It's challenging to go out amongst the "wolves" and be tested in our resolve to faithfully magnify God. This may even be, and often is, amongst our own family. Our desire for sainthood is really challenged in how we interact with people who aren't trying to serve the Lord.

What God told St. Catherine in *The Dialogue* passage shows us that when other people are unfaithful or hopeless, *that* is when we make the difference. When people are condescending, mean, or negative toward us, we are called to love and serve them. We are especially called to a mission of love in the world. It may seem like we are unqualified or unprepared to be the missionary disciples we are called to be, yet just by living the virtues and staying rooted in prayerful discernment, we can give witness to the love God has for us. The Holy Spirit will place us where we need to be to serve the Lord, so let us keep a zealous heart!

Do you act different around people of faith and those still yet to believe in God? How is your joy affected by your setting? Does your day-to-day life, and what you spend time thinking about, reflect that you want to be a saint? What does zeal mean to you? Consider adding "Walk on Water" by Britt Nicole to your prayer today.

ZEAL: DAY 60

This passage from *The Dialogue* encourages us in our different states of life, different vocations, and different gifts, but reminds us to live out all virtues.

[...] Her loving charity benefits herself first of all, as I have told you, when she conceives that virtue from which she draws the life of grace. Blessed with this unitive love she reaches out in loving charity to the whole world's need for salvation. But beyond a general love for all people she sets her eye on the specific needs of her neighbors and come to the aid of those nearest her according to the graces I have given her for minister: some she teaches by word, giving sincere and impartial counsel; others she teaches be her example--as everyone ought to--edifying her neighbors be her good, holy, honorable life. These are the virtues, with innumerable others, that are brought to birth in love of neighbor. But why have I established such differences? Why do I give this person one virtue and that person another, rather than giving them all to one person? It is true that all the virtues are bound together, and it is impossible to have one without having them all. But I give them in different ways so that one virtue might be, as it were, the source of all the others. So to one person I give charity as the primary virtue, to another justice, to another humility, to another a lively faith or prudence or temperance or patience, and to still another courage. These and many other virtues I give differently to different souls, and the soul is most at ease with that virtue which has been made primary for her. But through her love of that virtue she attracts all the other virtues to herself since they are all bound together in loving charity. *(St. Catherine of Siena. The Dialogue* (1980) Paulist Press)

God told St. Catherine that while we each have a primary virtue, we will begin to practice all the virtues because of love. Our zeal within that virtue brings us to the doorstep of the others. We have surely noticed over the past few weeks that each virtue is related to the others; they all help the others grow stronger. Our primary virtue is God's gift to us but isn't meant only for ourselves. We are not our own; we are made for relationship.

In the current culture with tee shirts proclaiming, "own your power," "my own boss," "girls rule the world," and other mantra's like "stop apologizing" we must recall Who made us and Who is the source of Good. Yes, we do have our unique gifts and talents, our charisms, our specific vocation and own way of evangelizing; but upon recognizing them, we humbly "reach out in loving charity" rather than turning our skills and preferences into idols. We don't seek praise for our personalities and lifestyles. We give all glory to God.

The important key for Christian women to combat the prideful and false "neo-feminist" mantras in the secular world is to recall that God is never supposed to be "in balance" with everything else in our life. The glory of God must flood every corner of our lives. That's the very definition of Him being our Lord. He's everywhere and sees everything, so we live our lives accordingly. We don't turn our femininity into an idol.

Our soul must be rightly directed toward His Goodness and our active life must be stacked appropriately behind the virtues. Jesus never commanded us to care about ourselves first, but He loves us enough to give us others to love too. Everyone around us has equal dignity, and we can't trample over it through a pursuit of power and control; in fact, we want to magnify the Lord so that others recognize their own dignity!

What is your primary virtue, the one where you feel most at ease? How do the other virtues flow out from it in your life? If it's helpful for you, journal or make a concept map connecting your soul to God and others through the virtues you recognize you practice. Where do other virtues need to grow?

ZEAL: DAY 61

Speaking up for God's Truth and living a totally Christian life will cause some to call us *Jesus freaks*. And they don't intend it as a compliment. But when we rid ourselves of our attachment to what people think of us, we will feel it is one.

For she grieves more over the offense done to me and the harm done to the other than over her own hurt. This is how those behave who are very perfect, and so they grow. And this is why I permit all these things. I grant them a stinging hunger for the salvation of souls so that they knock day and night at the door of my mercy, so much so that they forget themselves. And the more they abandon themselves, the more they find me. And where do they seek me? In my Truth, by walking perfectly along the way of his [Jesus] gentle teaching. *(St. Catherine of Siena. The Dialogue (1980) Paulist Press)*

Those whom I love, I reprove and chasten; so be zealous and repent.
– Revelation 3:19

For the grace of God has appeared for the salvation of all men, training us to renounce irreligion and worldly passions, and to live sober, upright, and godly lives in this world, awaiting our blessed hope, the appearing of the glory of our great God and Savior Jesus Christ, who gave himself for us to redeem us from all iniquity and to purify for himself a people of his own who are zealous for good deeds.
– Titus 2:11-14

God told St. Catherine that as we grow in holiness, we will care more about offenses against Him and the "least of His people" than we will about our own pains. How our hearts long for reverence of God! Our souls cry when we see someone carelessly receive our Lord in the Blessed Sacrament or He's left alone in the adoration chapel. We grieve over the offense against the Lord's intention for marriage, new life, end of life, or dignity of all lives.

Zeal for souls means we encourage others to rise to virtue, but of course we don't fall into vice to reach them. We cut off worldly desires to dress a certain way for our own vanity or to draw attention to ourselves. We need to say no to playing games, watching shows, or taking part in other activities that have occasions for sin or crude obscenities, or obsessing about TV or sports. We say no to gossip girl groups and drinking to get drunk. We've got to stop distracting ourselves from the Truth. God calls us to more. It's time to own up to personal responsibility out of zeal, sisters.

Our feminine genius will pursue virtue, not self-reliance; it will seek the good of others over ourselves. We care about consoling the Heart of Jesus when others make themselves a god and pursue their pleasure at the expense of their soul. We offer reparation for sins. Even more so, we notice our own imperfections, for even the slightest sin causes a wound in Christ's body. The closer we get to God, the more we notice our shortcomings. Monthly confession (or more frequently if needed) becomes a devotion, and the graces poured out support our zeal.

We let God perfect us through discipline and self-accusation. Are we really living counter-culturally? Yes, we are called to find common ground with others so that we can evangelize, but this looks like giving our time to be present with others, to walk with them, to share brokenness, and to shed the light that God shines through us now. We shouldn't engage in the sins others are struggling with in the name of "encounter". God grants eternal life only to those who thirst for it, and He sees through hypocrisy.

Do you think you can get to Heaven without thirsting for God and the souls of others? How does your life reflect this? Where else do you visit a worldly "well" to satiate your thirst? Read Luke 12:4-11.

(If you don't mind some Christian rap, Toby Mac's old band, DC Talk, has an old song, "Jesus Freak" that's in line with today's reflection)

ZEAL: DAY 62

We are growing in virtue so that we can be holy—and we are meant to be holy. Therefore, growing in virtue is what we are meant to do, and it will set the world on fire—with the Lord!

[Someone is] said to be zealous on God's behalf, when [s]he endeavors, to the best of [her] his means, to repel whatever is contrary to the honor or will of God; according to 1 Kings 19:14: "With zeal I have been zealous for the Lord of hosts." Again on the words of John 2:17: "The zeal of Thy house hath eaten me up," …
– *St. Thomas Aquinas, Summa Theologiae I-II, 28 4co*

Let love be sincere; hate what is evil, hold on to what is good; love one another with mutual affection; anticipate one another in showing honor. Do not grow slack in zeal, be fervent in spirit, serve the Lord. – *Romans 12:9-11*

I want to cast fire upon the earth; and would that it were already kindled!
– *Luke 12: 49*

"This lukewarmness proceeds from ingratitude, which comes from a faint light that does not let us see the agonizing and utter love of Christ crucified, and the infinite benefits received from Him. For in truth, did we see them, our heart would burn with the flame of love, and we should be famished for time, using it with great zeal for the honor of God and the salvation of souls. To this zeal I summon thee, dearest son, that now we begin to work anew… Do thou be fervent and not tepid in this activity... *If you are what you ought to be, you will set fire to all Italy, and without much cost.*"
– St. Catherine of Siena *(St. Catherine of Siena as Seen in Her Letters* (1905) EP Dutton & Co*)*

It's up to us to seek out virtue, and through that, we live our love in action—our zeal. Every moment is a chance to choose love. When we don't, let us repent and be grateful for mercy. Not being grateful, as St. Catherine says, will keep us lukewarm.

In this day and age, it's increasingly harder to distinguish lukewarm Catholic lives from purely secular lives, and it's the virtue of zeal that will shine the Light against the dim gray blending between "sort of religious" and complete paganism. St. Catherine of Siena is as radical as St. John the Baptist—different missions and different times, but just as zealous. She walked around telling people to repent and she didn't care who thought she was crazy. Her most popular quote is often rendered as "Be who God made you to be and you will set the world on fire." The actual translation seen above comes from a letter she wrote to her spiritual son, one of her scribes, Stefano. She was trying to convince him to live a bolder, more zealous life, to inspire the whole country to enflame their hearts as Jesus asked for the world to be ablaze. She was hoping to convict him against lukewarmness, not preaching a message of individualism as it's so often portrayed today.

How do we set the world ablaze? This is a question for meditative prayer. We prayerfully discern God's will in our life and then as St. Thomas Aquinas says, we repel what isn't the will of God.

One thing for sure though, we must contemplate the passion of Christ. The cross will always draw us into love. Does perfection against sin sound impossible? Sure. Let's admit we can never get there, but God can lift us up when we carry our cross in union with His.

When have you experienced joy by turning from sin? How do you feel called to enflame your heart? What "crazy" thing can you do for God today? Enthusiastically start fresh after this prayer time. You always have a choice to kindle the fire or put it out. Do you have someone in your life that encourages you to be virtuous? Thank God for His light in them. Add "Start a Fire" by Unspoken as part of your prayer if you want.

ZEAL: DAY 63

Zeal must be supported by other virtues; the genius of women is that we are receptive to God's call, sensitive to how emotions and actions play into virtue, and we are generous with our gifts. We can magnify the Lord through our strength and dignity.

Strength and dignity are her clothing, and she laughs at the time to come. She opens her mouth with wisdom, and the teaching of kindness is on her tongue. She looks well to the ways of her household, and does not eat the bread of idleness. Her children rise up and call her happy; her husband too, and he praises her: "Many women have done excellently, but you surpass them all." Charm is deceitful, and beauty is vain, but a woman who fears the Lord is to be praised. Give her a share in the fruit of her hands, and let her works praise her in the city gates.
– *Proverbs 31:26-31*

"A soul rises up, restless with tremendous desire for God's honor and the salvation of souls. She has for some time exercised herself in virtue and has become accustomed to dwelling in the cell of self-knowledge in order to know better God's goodness toward her, since upon knowledge follows love. And loving, she seeks to pursue truth and clothe herself in it." – St. Catherine of Siena *(St. Catherine of Siena as Seen in Her Letters* (1905) EP Dutton & Co*)*

As long as these three pillars (impurity, bloated pride, and greed) are standing upright and are not overthrown by the force of love of virtue, they are strong enough to keep the soul obstinately set in every other vice. *(St. Catherine of Siena. The Dialogue* (1980) Paulist Press*)*

When we connect the Proverbs scripture with what St. Catherine wrote, it proves to be a very good overarching benchmark to check how refined our virtue of zeal is. Are we courageous, pure, and aware of our dignity? Are we kind in teaching the truth? Are we "small-souled" or are we magnanimous? Are we slothful and wasteful of our time? Are we joyful? Are we vain or two-faced? Do we fear the Lord? Are we loving in our deeds?

Some of the biggest struggles with zeal may be our fear of being called "holier-than-thou," our feeling of being unqualified, or our concern that others just won't even care. But we can't care what other people call us or how they judge us—we live for one *final* judgement. Apathy by others is not an excuse; we are responsible for each other to the extent that we do or don't try to share the Gospel! It really doesn't matter if others are apathetic. We can have a friendship with them, and God will work in His own time. (If we prayerfully discern it's time to "shake the dust on our feet" and move on, so be it, but we must first try.) And finally, we can't care about being unqualified, God gives us the necessities to do the job He calls us to.

When we want to be that soul rising up to God like St. Catherine wrote about, we remember that it is He who gives us the grace to be lifted, we only have a light because it is He in us. We must keep our zeal balanced with reverence for God. He directs our steps.

Consider

Do you think zeal is planting or harvesting? How do you connect magnanimity and industriousness with zeal? What differences and similarities are there in working hard for the Glory of God and loving for the Glory of God? When have you been zealous but it seemed your efforts were fruitless? Does seeing or not seeing fruit affect our call as Christians? Consider adding Brandon Heath's "Lighthouse" as part of your prayer.

WEEKLY REFLECTIONS

Meekness & Patience

St. Teresa Benedicta of the Cross (Edith Stein)

WEEK 10 -
MEEKNESS & PATIENCE
St. Teresa Benedicta of the Cross (Edith Stein)

Mortifications	S	M	T	W	T	F	S
DAILY PRAYER (30 MIN) MAGNIFICAT, LITANY, ROSARY	✝	✝	✝	✝	✝	✝	✝
DAILY MASS							
CONFESSION (MONTHLY)							
ADORATION (WEEKLY)							
NO MAKEUP		✝			✝		
MEATLESS FASTING					✝		
INTENTIONAL WALK WITH FRIEND OR HUSBAND							
CONNECT WITH PERSON WHO CAME TO MIND IN PRAYER							
OTHER:							
OTHER:							
OTHER:							

Other Daily Mortifications to Remember

- ONLY CHRISTIAN/CLASSICAL MUSIC AND PODCASTS
- ONLY RELIGIOUS PROGRAMMING IN MODERATION
- NO WEIGHING ON A SCALE
- NO SWEETS, ALCOHOL, OR SNACKS IN BETWEEN MEALS
- NO SOCIAL MEDIA
- NO UNNECESSARY SHOPPING
- _____
- _____
-

I am offering my intentions for:

S ● _____
M ● _____
T ● _____
W ● _____
T ● _____
F ● _____
S ● _____
Other ● _____

Express Use this space to journal, draw, or otherwise express your thoughts on this week's virtue. Spend some time listening to the Holy Spirit, perhaps in Adoration, and capture whatever He brings to mind or lays on your heart.

MEEKNESS & PATIENCE: DAY 64

We reflect on meekness this week, a minor virtue under temperance; and patience, which falls under fortitude. The Beatitude pertaining to meekness is very similar to Psalm 37:

Be still before the Lord and wait patiently for him; fret not yourself over him who prospers in his way, over the man who carries out evil devices! Refrain from anger and forsake wrath! Fret not yourself; it tends only to evil. For the wicked shall be cut off; but those who wait for the Lord shall possess the land. Yet a little while, and the wicked will be no more; though you look well at his place, he will not be there. But the meek shall possess the land and delight themselves in abundant prosperity.
– Psalm 37: 7-11

CCC 716: The People of the "poor" (see Zephaniah 2:3; Psalm 22:27; 34:3; Isaiah 49:13; 61:1) - those who, humble and meek, rely solely on their God's mysterious plans, who await the justice, not of men but of the Messiah - are in the end the great achievement of the Holy Spirit's hidden mission during the time of the promises that prepare for Christ's coming. It is this quality of heart, purified and enlightened by the Spirit, which is expressed in the Psalms. In these poor, the Spirit is making ready "a people prepared for the Lord." (Luke 1:17)

Blessed are the meek, for they shall inherit the earth. *– Matthew 5:5*

Both a beatitude and a virtue, meekness stops anger from turning into wrath—it gives us gentleness in our reactions. It falls under the major virtue of temperance, because it moderates or balances dismissive attitudes with brutal ones. Meekness is the moderator of anger that isn't righteous, while patience helps us accept our crosses rather than running from them—to carry them if they are our path to holiness. If we fear being an angry person, we may go to the other extreme of forgetting our own dignity as daughters of God. So we also need fortitude because we can't enable sins or irresponsibility of others. Meekness is not weakness, as some in society may say. Meekness is a balance between being a "doormat" and being a cruel-outburst person. It also takes moral courage to go against the cultural tide of caring for ourselves first and treating others as less worthy. That moral courage of meekness is supported through patience, calmly waiting for God's perfect will to be revealed. So meekness can be thought of as what patience looks like externally.

The two minor virtues are quite intertwined because the crosses we need to patiently carry are often the ones that occur when others make us feel disrespected, ridiculed, or unjustly burdened (all of which are the source of anger for most people).

Surely what others say or do to us can, and often does, offend us. Trying to argue with our older children, neighbors, or even our aging parents will not be nearly as effective as intentional conversations poured forth from a humble and gentle soul (see Ephesians 4:15). We seek to magnify the Lord and bring Him glory by our meek responses to outrage (see John 8).

We can try to do everything on our own, or we can restrain our pride and strength appropriately with meekness. God's plans for us unfold in the best way to lead us to sainthood despite our concupiscence (see Romans 8:28). Grudges and resentment will always steal energy away from joy. Entitlement may very well be the undoing of many souls. It can chain us to our own inflating prideful attitude, reducing our virtue—most especially our patience and calmness of soul.

 **Think about times you have fixated on how someone has wronged you. How did you stay meek and patient, magnifying the Lord? How did you lash out? Did you withdraw and harbor resentment? How can your call to meekness as a virtue change the way you prepare for situations and relationships that you know push you to the edge?**

MEEKNESS & PATIENCE: DAY 65

Philosopher Edith Stein, known as St. Teresa Benedicta of the Cross was a life-long learner who will lead our feminine genius reflections into meekness and patience.

"Every time I feel my powerlessness and inability to influence people directly, I become more keenly aware of the necessity of my own holocaust." – St. Teresa Benedicta of the Cross (*Teresa Benedict of the Cross Edith Stein. Vatican biography:* https://www.vatican.va/news_services/liturgy/saints/ns_lit_doc_19981011_edith_stein_en.html)

"Let go of your plans. The first hour of your morning belongs to God. Tackle the day's work that he charges you with, and he will give you the power to accomplish it." – St. Teresa Benedicta of the Cross Edith Stein. *Essays on Woman: The Collected Works of Edith Stein.* (2012) ICS Publications)

"They must die with Christ in order to rise with Him: the lifelong death of suffering and of daily self-denial..." – St. Teresa Benedicta of the Cross (Edith Stein. *The Science of the Cross.* (2002) ICS Publications)

Before her conversion, Edith Stein was a Jewish-turned-atheist woman living in the early 1900s. She read St. Teresa of Avila's biography and soon after converted to Catholicism. She studied German and history but was much more interested in philosophy, eventually writing a dissertation about empathy. She focused her studies on womanhood and how women have a lot to contribute to active society because of their people-focused intellects. She recognized that women are "mothers" to more than just their children. Women are interested in the continuation of society simply for the good of the world, not for a hidden agenda; they often teach not out of pride, but out of a desire to grow the community (the maternity and generosity pieces of the feminine genius). As a childless woman herself, she was especially qualified to speak on this topic for all women.

Edith Stein exemplified meekness because she could have had any number of angry reactions to her situations but sought to do God's will alone. She restrained her personal will, strong as it was, because she wanted God to make her holy. Patience is acceptance and trust in involuntary sufferings— particularly when people or situations make us disappointed. As a teacher of philosophy, Edith Stein was denied professorship based on her womanhood and then later on her "Jewishness." She still carried on her writing and influenced those around her by drawing near to the Truth of Christ at a time when it was punishable by death in many places.

Patience looks like denying ourselves instant gratification. Her spiritual director told Edith Stein not to enter a convent for various reasons, despite her wish to enter a Carmelite convent. She was patient with God's plan for her and spent time sharing Christ with her family and those around her. Her sister did convert as a result of that time spent together, and both entered a convent as the second World War broke out.

As indicated by her taking the religious name "Blessed of the Cross," she found herself greatly attached to Christ's passion. Recognizing that Christ called us all to take up our cross and follow Him (Matthew 16:24), she practiced the virtues of meekness and patience in the face of challenges and injustice. She was very interested in nonviolence and in perpetuating Christ's mission of love. To repay injury with calm peace, to suffer willingly with patience…these were her final testimonies. St. Teresa Benedicta was smuggled from one Carmelite convent to another during Nazi oppression, but was found and taken to a concentration camp, where she was quickly sent to the gas chambers. Her writings and ideas lived on and now are some of the most cited in the framework of feminine genius spirituality.

Our desire to help others encounter Jesus means that we must be witnesses to His love, mercy, and sacrifice that ties together joy in Him. Our own love, mercy, and sacrifice is exhibited obviously in meekness—when people insult or hurt us and we respond with love. This witness is more powerful than words. We can't save people or always influence their faith, but we can bear our crosses like Christ and trust in Him.

Are you a planner? Are you free to be directed by God's will? How does trust enable meekness and patience to flourish? How would being a little meeker and a little more patient help your sacrifices and sufferings bring you closer to becoming a Saint? Do you see any connections between generosity and meekness?

MEEKNESS & PATIENCE: DAY 66

When we allow our crosses to be "yoked" to Jesus, our soul is more peaceful, and we live out the virtues that we are to emulate. When we are faithful to Him, we live in the world, but we know we aren't home.

Take my yoke upon you, and learn from me; for I am gentle and lowly in heart, and you will find rest for your souls. – *Matthew 11:29*

For the fear of the Lord is wisdom and instruction, and he delights in fidelity and meekness. – *Sirach 1:27*

"Even now I accept the death that God has prepared for me in complete submission and with joy as being his most holy will for me. I ask the Lord to accept my life and my death ... so that the Lord will be accepted by His people and that His Kingdom may come in glory, for the salvation of Germany and the peace of the world" – *St. Teresa Benedicta of the Cross's will and testament June 9, 1938*

Upon her canonization, Pope St. John Paul II called St. Teresa Benedicta, "a daughter of Israel who, as a Catholic during Nazi persecution, remained faithful to the crucified Lord Jesus Christ and, as a Jew, to her people in loving faithfulness." *http://www.vatican.va/news_services/liturgy/saints/ns_lit_doc_19981011_edith_stein_en.html*

In some translations Matthew 11:29 reads "meek" instead of "gentle," and "humble" instead of "lowly." These four words speak to peacefulness, a peace the world cannot give. The Lord wants to give us calmness of soul, peaceful spirits. If we "fear the Lord," we pay attention to His commands and instructions; if we align our will with His will, then we will be virtuous—we will be saints.

St. Teresa Benedicta so beautifully wrote how it is possible to look at where we want to be and use where we are now to find joy on earth—through being yoked to Christ. Let this be our meditation for today;

> **But because being one with Christ is our sanctity, and progressively becoming one with Him our happiness on earth, the love of the cross in no way contradicts being a joyful child of God. Helping Christ carry his cross fills one with a strong and pure joy, and those who may and can do so, the builders of God's kingdom, are the most authentic children of God. And so those who have a predilection [fondness] for the Way of the Cross by no means deny that Good Friday is past and that the work of salvation has been accomplished. Only those who are saved, only children of grace, can in fact be bearers of Christ's cross. Only in union with the divine Head does human suffering take on expiatory power.**

To suffer and to be happy although suffering, to have one's feet on the earth, to walk on the dirty and rough paths of this earth and yet to be enthroned with Christ at the Father's right hand, to laugh and cry with the children of this world and ceaselessly to sing the praises of God with the choirs of angels, this is the life of the Christian until the morning of eternity breaks forth. ("At the Foot of the Cross: Love of the Cross: Some Thoughts for the Feast of St. John of the Cross" – St. Teresa Benedicta of the Cross (*The Hidden Life Hagiographic Essays, Meditations, Spiritual Texts* (1992) ICS Publications)

How does what we do on Earth illuminate what Christ did here? Are we becoming one with Him here? Do we carry our cross? He died and rose again. Have we died to ourselves? Have we risen to a new life on earth? Do we live differently as we "progressively become one with Christ"? How does the Eucharist encompass this theme?

If you'd like, include "The Cost" by Rend Collective as a part of your prayer.

MEEKNESS & PATIENCE: DAY 67

St. Teresa Benedicta sought unity with God so deeply that she neglected the world at first, thinking the spiritual life was suppressed by the world. She came to realize we must sanctify our life *in* the world, not run from it. Virtue helps our cross be sanctifying.

I therefore, a prisoner for the Lord, beg you to lead a life worthy of the calling to which you have been called, with all lowliness and meekness, with patience, forbearing one another in love, eager to maintain the unity of the Spirit in the bond of peace. There is one body and one Spirit, just as you were called to the one hope that belongs to your call, one Lord, one faith, one baptism, one God and Father of us all, who is above all and through all and in all. – *Ephesians 4:1-6*

"The soul of woman must be so expansive and open to all human beings [receptive], it must be quiet so that no small weak flame will be extinguished by stormy winds; warm so as not to benumb fragile buds [sensitive]….empty of itself in order that extraneous life may have room in it [maternal]; finally mistress of itself and also of its body so that the entire person is readily at the disposal of every call [generous]."
– *St. Teresa Benedicta* (notes added for pointing out feminine genius qualities) (Edith Stein. *Essays on Woman: The Collected Works of Edith Stein.* (2012) ICS Publications*)*

"I even believe that the deeper someone is drawn to God, the more she has to 'get beyond himself' in this sense, that is, go into the world and carry divine life into it."
– *St. Teresa Benedicta of the Cross (Edith Stein. The Science of the Cross. (2002) ICS Publications)*

Trying to develop meekness may incline us to avoid conflict all together. However, conflict and its subsequent resolution can actually lead us to unity, while avoidance of conflict creates an illusion of unity that will eventually boil over to something as big as schism.

When we want to retreat from the weight of the world, let us take St. Teresa's words to heart; we are called to carry divine life into it! When others hurt us, we don't fire back. We calmly and meekly respond by what most helps others see the face of God's mercy and love.

As we encounter a hurting neighbor, a lonely friend, or a lost soul, we walk with them as a companion. We seek to magnify the Lord so that others are drawn into His embrace. Our ever-loving Father wishes to see all His children find true joy and transcendent happiness in Him—and He uses us to reflect that when we respond meekly. The feminine genius spirituality anchors a woman, giving us pillars from which our faith builds a house, full of hope and love that welcomes others in. Our creation was for union with God and with other humans who are made in His image. We can't avoid conflict, because we all have our own opinions and sins, but going through the struggles within ourselves and with others can bring us deeper into the love of Christ.

Consider

What is necessary to restore unity? Within the global Church, how can meekness help? Within your local church, what will bring more unity? What about in your own family? If, for a time, that is conflict, how can the desire for unity guide our discussions and resolutions of disagreements? Again, we can't control others or give them faith or virtue, but we can do our best to keep communication open and charitable.

Also, do you ever want to avoid conflict? Do you want to avoid the world often? Connect meekness and patience with affability that we reflected on in the beginning of our 90 days. Who in your life needs your meekness?

MEEKNESS & PATIENCE: DAY 68

DAY 68: Beatitude means supreme blessedness. We can particularly recall *blessed are the meek for they shall inherit the earth*. It's possible to begin our sharing in divine life here as St. Teresa writes about, even if we don't consider ourselves mystics.

CCC 1717: The Beatitudes depict the countenance of Jesus Christ and portray his charity. They express the vocation of the faithful associated with the glory of his Passion and Resurrection; they shed light on the actions and attitudes characteristic of the Christian life; they are the paradoxical promises that sustain hope in the midst of tribulations; they proclaim the blessings and rewards already secured, however dimly, for Christ's disciples; they have begun in the lives of the Virgin Mary and all the saints.

1721: God put us in the world to know, to love, and to serve him, and so to come to paradise. Beatitude makes us "partakers of the divine nature" and of eternal life. (2 Peter 1:4) With beatitude, man enters into the glory of Christ (Romans 8:18) and into the joy of the Trinitarian life.

"The highest perfection to which a created spirit may attain—but, to be sure, not without divine aid—is the beatific vision. This is the divine gift of union with God by which the created spirit partakes of divine knowledge in sharing divine life. [...] The mystical vision or mystical union represents the closest approximation to this highest goal that is attainable in this earthly life. A preliminary stage, however, for which this highest favor is not required, is a true and living faith." – *St. Teresa Benedicta of the Cross (Finite and Eternal Being: An Attempt at an Ascent to the Meaning of Being (2002) ICS Publications)*

Grace gives us the ability to grow into union with the Divine through our virtuous life and our contemplative prayer. The Holy Spirit gives us power to have self-control (recall our meditation last week). We have the ability to be free from letting our passions drive us to false gods. This power to be "self-controlled" means a meek woman isn't a slave to her emotions or attached to her own reputation or self-esteem. As written earlier this week, meekness tempers our anger and reactions.

We don't put down others, gossip, or mock them; despite other's sins, we must love them mercifully as Christ's example shows us. Even if we disagree with someone, we can't hold grudges or seek retribution. We don't shut people out of our life in response to anger. And if we have any blame in an argument or dysfunction, we seek forgiveness and make amends. Self-accusation is an examining of what we could do better to listen to others and hear their sincere needs from us that would help them see God's Goodness.

Relationships are where God asks us to show love, so even if we hate the sins of others, we speak His Truth in such a way that others know we see their dignity and desire their salvation as much as we do our own. Whatever choice we make to handle a challenging dynamic, let us pray that we patiently do God's will—always discerning relationships, as our experience within them is a chance to magnify the Lord.

Consider

Take some time to journal or reflect on areas where lack of meekness keeps you from a "true and living faith", missing the entry into a state of supreme blessedness as quoted from St. Teresa. How do you fall prey to the desire to have the last word or desire to be acknowledged, correct, liked, or respected at all costs (recall our+? Do you feel offended when others challenge your status quo? What do you think God is asking you to do, say, or be in your most difficult relationship? Include "Song of my Father" by Urban Rescue as part of your prayer today, if you'd like.

MEEKNESS & PATIENCE: DAY 69

Meekness serves to keep anger holy, therefore it is a virtue opposed to wrath. Patience is a virtue because it endures wrongs and dulls concupiscence.

For anger, which is mitigated by meekness, is, on account of its impetuousness, a very great obstacle to [wo]man's free judgment of truth: wherefore meekness above all makes a [wo]man self-possessed. – *St. Thomas Aquinas, Summa Theologiae II-II, Q157, co4*

Wherefore Augustine says (De Patientia ii): "A man's patience it is whereby he bears evil with an equal mind," i.e. without being disturbed by sorrow, "lest he abandon with an unequal mind the goods whereby he may advance to better things." It is therefore evident that patience is a virtue. – *St. Thomas Aquinas, Summa Theologiae II-II, Q136, co1*

You have heard that it was said, 'An eye for an eye and a tooth for a tooth.' But I say to you, do not resist one who is evil. But if anyone strikes you on the right cheek, turn to him the other also; and if anyone would sue you and take your coat, let him have your cloak as well; and if anyone forces you to go one mile, go with him two miles. Give to him who begs from you, and do not refuse him who would borrow from you. – *Matthew 5:38-42*

"If anyone comes to me, I want to lead them to Him." – *St. Teresa Benedicta* (https://www.vatican.va/news_services/liturgy/saints/ns_lit_doc_19981011_edith_stein_en.html)

When we try to grow in meekness as a virtue, we trust God to turn offense against us into something greater. Hope of Heaven – the Beatific Vision – helps ward off self-pity or despair because we know no joy comes from having a chip on our shoulder. We live our lives asking God to purify our souls into the Saints we are called to be, and we extend mercy generously to others because it brings us true and lasting joy.

We should never choose to suffer pain, rebuke, insult, or injury as an end in itself. We only endure them patiently and respond out of meekness, because they are opportunities to combat sin—that is, separation from God—through unity with His passion, death, and resurrection. As we've reflected on before, virtues are not the end all be all…. they are the way to magnify the Lord in the world through our own lives. Our virtues lead us and others to Him.

We can't be like the secular culture that seeks retribution and "fairness" in the vein of selfish pride (see CCC 2485). What is fair, what is just to God—humility, peacefulness, gentleness—these are to be held in high esteem. Tranquility of soul leads to unmovable joy anchored in love. Think of the words we use to describe Mary, our model in Magnify: blessed, gentle, meek, humble, full of joy. To obtain these traits in our life, we need to actively pursue virtue.

Consider

Read this passage from CCC 2843: "...the heart that offers itself to the Holy Spirit turns injury into compassion and purifies the memory in transforming the hurt into intercession."

Take the readings above and this Catechism passage to prayer and journal. If necessary, make steps to offer your heart to the Holy Spirit, turn hurt into intercession. Consider reaching out in compassion to someone that offended you, not because you anticipate an apology, but because it gives you internal freedom to be united with Love.

MEEKNESS & PATIENCE: DAY 70

Patience and meekness bring us to our unique fiat, our "yes" to God's will for our life. The maternity piece of our feminine genius is found in all vocations and best modeled by Mary.

But even if you do suffer for righteousness' sake, you will be blessed. Have no fear of them, nor be troubled, but in your hearts reverence Christ as Lord. Always be prepared to make a defense to anyone who calls you to account for the hope that is in you, yet do it with gentleness and reverence; and keep your conscience clear, so that, when you are abused, those who revile your good behavior in Christ may be put to shame. For it is better to suffer for doing right, if that should be God's will, than for doing wrong. – *1 Peter 3:14-17*

"Both spiritual companionship and spiritual motherliness are not limited to the physical wife and mother relationship, but they extend to all people with whom woman comes into contact."

"Every profession in which woman's soul comes into its own and which can be formed by woman's soul is an authentic woman's profession."

"To be a mother is to nourish and protect humanity and bring it to development."

– St. Teresa Benedicta on various vocations and states in life for women (Edith Stein Essays on Woman: The Collected Works of Edith Stein. (2012) ICS Publications)

Meekness and patience require humility, gratitude, and docility. Like Mary, we must seek to say "yes" to God while magnifying Him in our soul. This brings maturity to our spirituality of maternity. If the call to be a zealous feminine genius in the world seems exhausting, we recall how our weakness leads us to dwelling in God's mercy.

St. Teresa Benedicta's profound words have given encouragement to faith-filled women seeking their place in the contentious landscape of gender identity, fluidity, and denial in the modern world. Authentic womanhood is under attack. We hear the neo-feminist insistence that to be valued, we must be able to do everything men do and do away with gender distinction. Yet by many we are viewed as weaker and often respected less no matter what we do or what achievements we claim.

Through acknowledging the the unity of Most Holy Trinity, we come to understand that the answer to our longing and respect for our dignity is not based on what we do. It comes from who we are— women! God calls each woman to a unique vocation that utilizes our femininity. Many of us are called to work in the world while many others are called to physical motherhood through birth or adoption. We can be called to both—or neither, if God draws us into a relationship with Him through a vocation to consecrated life. The paths for living our life are as varied as each of us. It comes down to discerning God's will and following it. When we chase what isn't our vocation, we find ourselves unfulfilled, imbalanced, and disheartened.

Perhaps we are tempted by something different than our true vocation and opinions of others, or our expectations of what life should look like weigh heavy on us. Temptation may make us feel our intellect is wasted when we stay home to raise kids, or others snub us if we weren't called to have kids, or they act disappointed that we work full-time, or we feel neglected now that we are retired and live alone, or we are labeled "crazy" for living a consecrated life. How many of us ever feel inadequate or lost—like we don't fit into any one box nicely no matter what we do? We can't please everyone. The One to please is the Lord.

When we discern God's will for our life, we find that the only box we need to fit into is "holy." We must remember that we need to cling to the hope that we become Saints through our interior life of prayer, enriched by the sacraments that fortify our virtues of our active life.

What virtues help you maintain calmness despite pursuing a counter-cultural lifestyle? How do meekness and patience help you maintain hope in your vocation? Include "Just Give Me Jesus" by Unspoken if you'd like. Spend extra time in thanksgiving for the gift of sustenance in the Eucharist today.

WEEKLY REFLECTIONS

Foresight & Providence

St. Zélie Martin

WEEK 11 - FORESIGHT & PROVIDENCE
St. Zélie Martin

Mortifications	S	M	T	W	T	F	S
DAILY PRAYER (30 MIN) MAGNIFICAT, LITANY, ROSARY	✝	✝	✝	✝	✝	✝	✝
DAILY MASS							
CONFESSION (MONTHLY)							
ADORATION (WEEKLY)							
NO MAKEUP			✝			✝	
MEATLESS FASTING						✝	
INTENTIONAL WALK WITH FRIEND OR HUSBAND							
CONNECT WITH PERSON WHO CAME TO MIND IN PRAYER							
OTHER:							
OTHER:							
OTHER:							

Other Daily Mortifications to Remember

- ONLY CHRISTIAN/CLASSICAL MUSIC AND PODCASTS
- ONLY RELIGIOUS PROGRAMMING IN MODERATION
- NO WEIGHING ON A SCALE
- NO SWEETS, ALCOHOL, OR SNACKS IN BETWEEN MEALS
- NO SOCIAL MEDIA
- NO UNNECESSARY SHOPPING
- _____
- _____
- _____

I am offering my intentions for:

S ● _____
M ● _____
T ● _____
W ● _____
T ● _____
F ● _____
S ● _____
Other ● _____

Express Use this space to journal, draw, or otherwise express your thoughts on this week's virtue. Spend some time listening to the Holy Spirit, perhaps in Adoration, and capture whatever He brings to mind or lays on your heart.

FORESIGHT & PROVIDENCE: DAY 71

This week we reflect on foresight as a virtue vital to prudence. It is looking to the future with cautionary choices now. Divine Providence necessarily directs our use of prudence because we cannot virtuously think of the future without recognizing that God already knows. The words are all actually etymologically related.

CCC 306: God is the sovereign master of his plan. But to carry it out he also makes use of his creatures' co-operation. This use is not a sign of weakness, but rather a token of almighty God's greatness and goodness. For God grants his creatures not only their existence, but also the dignity of acting on their own, of being causes and principles for each other, and thus of co-operating in the accomplishment of his plan.

307: To human beings God even gives the power of freely sharing in his providence by entrusting them with the responsibility of "subduing" the earth and having dominion over it (see Gen 1:26-28). God thus enables men to be intelligent and free causes in order to complete the work of creation, to perfect its harmony for their own good and that of their neighbors. Though often unconscious collaborators with God's will, they can also enter deliberately into the divine plan by their actions, their prayers and their sufferings (see Colossians 1:24). They then fully become "God's fellow workers" and co-workers for his kingdom (see 1 Corinthians 3:9).

308: The truth that God is at work in all the actions of his creatures is inseparable from faith in God the Creator. God is the first cause who operates in and through secondary causes: "For God is at work in you, both to will and to work for his good pleasure." (Philippians 2:13) Far from diminishing the creature's dignity, this truth enhances it. Drawn from nothingness by God's power, wisdom and goodness, it can do nothing if it is cut off from its origin, for "without a Creator the creature vanishes." (GS 36 § 3) Still less can a creature attain its ultimate end without the help of God's grace (Matthew 19:26).

The secular understanding of foresight conveys a sense of precaution, or analysis of all possible outcomes. But as a virtue it has to do with seeing God as our source of life and making choices in authentic recognition of His love. The good that God wills for us is an eternity of freedom from sin—and we must be active participants in pursuit of this good (such as, accepting God's will) or else we effectively damn ourselves to hell.

Foresight helps us see ways we need to mortify ourselves to root out sin, so we become less attached to the world with each passing day. Foresight sometimes looks like knocking on metaphorical doors in our lives to see if they open to a path that draws us closer to God—then choosing another door if they don't.

We act prudently when we consider various options for an action or inaction, gather information about which is best, and then make and act on the correct choice. As we mature, this often happens quickly, or even instantaneously for small things.

Prudence is considered the primary virtue because we are trying to make what we consider to be "good" choices in the moment so that the future is better. This impacts all of our habits, our virtues. We must first be able to discern what good is and then make good choices; we can't be temperate in our consumption if we don't first know what is helpful or harmful to us. We can't be fair to others if we don't recognize what is fair. And we certainly can't have fortitude if we don't prudently determine the morals in which to persevere. We see prudence leads the pursuit of other cardinal virtues—but how we struggle to find traction within it when scrupulosity weighs us down or presumption pridefully urges us on.

Consider

As you have become more conscious of the way virtues affect your interior life, how have you moved from unconscious collaborator to a full co-worker? Reflect on your spiritual history; where has God helped you along the way even when life seemed hard or confusing? Why can you trust He knows better? How does meditative prayer inspire prudence? What other activities in your life help you grow in foresight?

FORESIGHT & PROVIDENCE: DAY 72

St. Zélie Martin was canonized with her husband, St. Louis Martin in 2015. St. Thérèse of Lisieux wrote this about her parents, whose virtues were based in providential spirituality, "Heaven is the place toward which all their actions and desires tended."

CCC 2046: By living with the mind of Christ, Christians hasten the coming of the Reign of God, "a kingdom of justice, love, and peace." (Roman Missal, Preface for Christ the King) They do not, for all that, abandon their earthly tasks; faithful to their master, they fulfill them with uprightness, patience, and love.

"If God wants to heal me, I would be very happy because deep down I want to live. It is costing me something to leave my husband and my children. But on the other hand, I say to myself, 'If I am not healed, it is because it would be perhaps more useful for them if I went away....'" – *St. Zélie Martin*

"I was like you when I started my lace business in Alençon. I made myself sick over it; now I am much more reasonable. I am less concerned and have resigned myself to the troublesome events that occur and that can happen to me. I tell myself that God permits this, and then I don't think about it anymore." – *St. Zélie Martin*

St. Zélie Martin was raised in a rigid family but grew into a meek woman of love, who had a trust in providence that gave her great foresight. Zélie desired a religious life vocation yet was turned away for health concerns. She discerned that God must be calling her to married life. While waiting for her vocation to come to fruition, she opened a lace business. This actually led to her meeting Louis, as his mother came to know Zélie through it and urged them to meet. Quickly after meeting they married. They had 9 children—five girls lived to adulthood and all became nuns—the most famous of all was St. Thérèse, the Little Flower.

Zélie was a *feminine genius* striving to live out a virtuous life—taking care of the poor, having compassion for her workers, staying close to the Lord in sacraments and prayer—while also encouraging all of those around her to become saints. She went to daily Mass, received Holy Communion as often as was allowed, and on most Sundays, she went to two or three Masses! She lived a life around the liturgical calendar including pilgrimages, retreats, and fasting when not pregnant (she acknowledged that she did not like fasting, nor did she consider herself "strong" enough to do it well). The Martin family also kept Sunday as a day of true rest, which was countercultural as France was increasingly less religious and more businesses were staying open on Sunday.

Louis sold his watch shop to take on assisting with the more successful family business of lace, run by Zélie — quite an example for discernment within marriage even if the path seemed radical to the world; a man supporting his wife's endeavors. The ways in which men and women are complementary within the vocation to marriage can be varied within the Providence of God. God can work in all ways to draw others to Him, so long as we are open and trusting of His will.

Her goal in raising her children was to help them become saints, and in turn, she herself became one. She was canonized for the way she lived out her vocation to married life—what hope this gives those of us called to marriage! We may often feel it isn't as pious as a consecrated life, but the only way to be a Saint is to follow God's will for our lives. Her choices about lifestyle, activities permitted, words and affirmations used (or not used), and passing on the faith led to the Martin family being able to thrive in her absence—because she taught them to be rooted in Christ and practice virtue to magnify the Lord.

Zélie died at 46 after years of battling breast cancer that metastasized. She suffered immensely—her descriptions of pain and trials memorialized in letters can still be read in various books about the family. Her calmness through her sufferings serve as a testament to a virtuous soul that knew Heaven is infinitely better than earth—and if God permits bodily death, it is so that more good can be brought from it. Her death brought her family even closer to God, provoking Thérèse to adopt Mary as her spiritual mother, and inspiring the great spirituality that the Little Flower passed on to all of us as a Doctor of the Church.

How can the example of St. Zélie remind you that it is living out your particular vocation that matters? How does foresight tie into your plans and goals for life, big or small? Are all your actions and desires tending toward Heaven? Why do you think discernment and foresight are related?

Foresight gives us the mindset to open a path for God to perfect us. We can reach true freedom from sin when we are attentive to areas we need to detach from.

My son, if you receive my words and treasure up my commandments with you, making your ear attentive to wisdom and inclining your heart to understanding; yes, if you cry out for insight and raise your voice for understanding, if you seek it like silver and search for it as for hidden treasures; then you will understand the fear of the Lord and find the knowledge of God. For the Lord gives wisdom; from his mouth come knowledge and understanding; he stores up sound wisdom for the upright; he is a shield to those who walk in integrity, guarding the paths of justice and preserving the way of his saints. Then you will understand righteousness and justice and equity, every good path; for wisdom will come into your heart, and knowledge will be pleasant to your soul; discretion will watch over you; understanding will guard you… *– Proverbs 2:1-11*

"In brief, I do not see things darkly, and that is a great grace that God has given me…… Whatever happens let's profit from the good times that remain and let's not worry ourselves. Besides, things will always be what God wants." *– St. Zélie Martin*

So you, by the help of your God, return, hold fast to love and justice, and wait continually for your God. *– Hosea 12: 6*

Turning foresight from a secular quality to a faith-filled spiritual virtue hinges on fear of the Lord. Fear of the Lord isn't being afraid of God. It is being in awe of Him, caring about Him so much that we don't want to be cut off from Him through consciously sinning. We try to understand what sin is, what leads us to sin, how to avoid sin; so, we seek wisdom and counsel. By welcoming the Holy Spirit in as our Counselor, by pursuing Truth, we can discern the will of God and try harder to avoid sin.

We want to know the fullness of God's will, but often He only reveals a little at a time: the next right step. A problem arises when we place too much emphasis on what's going to come around the next turn. Foresight is not predicting the future. The Bible passages and St. Zélie quote above remind us that if we stay close to God, the holiness is found in the waiting. Foresight actually requires patience. Yes, we must look to the future, but Jesus told His followers many times not to worry about tomorrow.

Our fear and anxiety about our future, or our children's future, or what will happen if this or that occurs (or doesn't) isn't virtuous. We can care about the future only to the extent that it brings us closer to God, and this keeps our soul in a state of journeying toward perfection via Providence. We make plans for the future recognizing them as a means to help us evangelize, encounter Christ in others, or draw us deeper into relationship with Him. We don't use foresight to set and achieve goals for their own end.

Consider

How much do you obsess over what you "need" to get done? How open are you to the promptings of the Holy Spirit? Does your planning grow your trust in God or distract from it? Does your schedule fill your time with pursuit of virtue or pursuit of worldly things like comfort, pleasure, power, and money? If God grants you wealth or power, do you use it for His glory? How can the Magnify 90 asceticism help you utilize prudence on the path toward holiness? Read Matthew 6:25-34 considering the virtue of foresight.

FORESIGHT & PROVIDENCE: DAY 74

God's permitted will is often hard to understand, yet we must continue to trust in Him and bear our crosses.

CCC 310: But why did God not create a world so perfect that no evil could exist in it? With infinite power God could always create something better. (see Aquinas ST I,25,6) But with infinite wisdom and goodness God freely willed to create a world "in a state of journeying" towards its ultimate perfection. In God's plan this process of becoming involves the appearance of certain beings and the disappearance of others, the existence of the more perfect alongside the less perfect, both constructive and destructive forces of nature. With physical good there exists also physical evil as long as creation has not reached perfection. (see Aquinas *Summa Contra Gentiles* III,71)

For the moment all discipline seems painful rather than pleasant; later it yields the peaceful fruit of righteousness to those who have been trained by it. Therefore lift your drooping hands and strengthen your weak knees, and make straight paths for your feet, so that what is lame may not be put out of joint but rather be healed. Strive for peace with all men, and for the holiness without which no one will see the Lord. – *Hebrews 12:11-14*

"The wisest thing, the simplest thing, in all this is to resign oneself to God's will and to prepare ahead of time to carry one's cross as bravely as possible."
– *St. Zélie Martin*

Bad things happen, sad things happen, *crosses* exist. Pain and suffering exist, but it's what we do with them that affects our path to becoming saints. God brings good out of them through His benevolent creative nature. God's infinite nature renders Him continually creative. He did not make the world already complete as evidenced by the fact that seasons change, people are born and die, and we grow in mind and body. It logically follows that the never-ending God would continue to create. We are made in His image, able to participate in creating as well. We are called to actively and freely choose good for others and ourselves. We all fall short of this perfection, so the world is full of disrupted nature, disrupted relationships, and disrupted order.

St. Zélie knew one of the most tragic pains a woman can endure: the pain of infant and child loss. Two sons and one daughter died as infants, and five-year-old Helene died after a heart-wrenching illness that caused difficulty breathing. These deaths truly tested Zélie's hope, faith, and love. She acknowledged it was good to have a child in Heaven interceding for her, but she also wrote about the grief and sadness she felt from the losses—saying she wasn't sure purgatory could be worse. Her virtues allowed her to see that God has good in store beyond our comprehension. She gives us the example that there is much to be done on earth: people to actively love, redemptive suffering to be offered, and peace and joy to be found in Christ. Continuing to participate in God's creative nature can help draw us out of ourselves. The situations God provides for us can make us saints if we cooperate.

Consider

How does reflecting on God's creation of the world in a state of journeying affect your view on pursuing sainthood? Think of a time that your peace and joy was disrupted by a worldly affliction or pain. How does your reflection on providence affect your foresight moving forward? If you'd like, add the song "Glorious Things" by Sarah & John McMillian as part of your prayer. In addition, you can read the Scripture verses it's based on: Psalm 87:3 and Ecclesiastes 3:11.

FORESIGHT & PROVIDENCE: DAY 75

Jesus came to unite us all; He asks that we love our neighbor as ourselves. When we are prudent, we can foresee ways that divide and ways that unite. We can have the hard conversations that don't sweep conflict under the rug. Providence provides opportunities to strengthen the body of believers through our own personal call to holiness.

CCC 2045: Because they are members of the Body whose Head is Christ (see Ephesians 1:22), Christians contribute to building up the Church by the constancy of their convictions and their moral lives. The Church increases, grows, and develops through the holiness of her faithful, until "we all attain to the unity of the faith and of the knowledge of the Son of God, to mature manhood, to the measure of the stature of the fullness of Christ." (Ephesians 4:13)

For the promise is to you and to your children and to all that are far off, every one whom the Lord our God calls to him." And he testified with many other words and exhorted them, saying, "Save yourselves from this crooked generation." So those who received his word were baptized, and there were added that day about three thousand souls. And they devoted themselves to the apostles' teaching and fellowship, to the breaking of bread and the prayers. – *Acts 2:39-42*

And Joshua said to the people, "Sanctify yourselves; for tomorrow the Lord will do wonders among you." – *Joshua 3:5*

"I want to be a saint." – *St. Zélie Martin*

As we consider Christian unity with our virtue of foresight, we can think of the early apostolic communities and of the Israelites coming out of Egypt with Moses and then Joshua. What can we learn from them? What have we lost in our communities today?

We remember the zeal of these groups, the desire to be God's people. By nature of our baptism into the Body of Christ, we are God's people too. We Christians should be bound together in our fellowship, our celebration of the Mass, and our day-to-day life. We are stronger in our virtues when we are elevated through holy friendships—iron sharpening iron.

It takes unity to convey Truth. If we are divided, the Gospel message entrusted to us deteriorates. People's belief falls apart under the weight of various cracks and divisions. Incongruity erupts, the "truth" becomes relative, and then many can't see Christ in the world.

Who holds you accountable for your pursuit of virtue? Do you have a spiritual director or mentor? Do you have spiritual friends that inspire your zeal? God created us for communion. To experience Him more fully on earth we need each other. Our zeal for souls should be unifying, not destructive or exclusionary. When we take our zeal and pair it with the prudence of foresight, we have an equation for holiness.

Consider

What are your thoughts on unity as it relates to foresight? Have you been a source of division within your parish and/or family? Have you tried to bring others together? How tightly do you cling to your own bubble of comfort—or do you invite strangers in? How is God asking you to get rid of the things or situations or choices impeding your sanctification through trusting in His Providence?

FORESIGHT & PROVIDENCE: DAY 76

St. Thérèse wrote: "As little birds learn to sing by listening to their parents, so children learn the science of virtues, the sublime song of Divine Love from souls responsible for forming them."

I consider that the sufferings of this present time are not worth comparing with the glory that is to be revealed to us. For the creation waits with eager longing for the revealing of the sons of God; for the creation was subjected to futility, not of its own will but by the will of him who subjected it in hope; because the creation itself will be set free from its bondage to decay and obtain the glorious liberty of the children of God. We know that the whole creation has been groaning in travail together until now; and not only the creation, but we ourselves, who have the first fruits of the Spirit, groan inwardly as we wait for adoption as sons, the redemption of our bodies. For in this hope we were saved. Now hope that is seen is not hope. For who hopes for what he sees? But if we hope for what we do not see, we wait for it with patience. – *Romans 8:18-25*

"We need to dispose ourselves to accept the will of the good Lord with open hearts, whatever it is, because His will is always what is best for us." – *St. Zélie Martin*

Because of our tendency to sin, our concupiscence, we humans have a "default setting" to view suffering as bad. We cannot deal with discomforts or past wounds by chasing luxuries or vanity and then expect our friends and family to see the Lord magnified in us. We can't turn to despair when the burdens of life weigh us down. We must trust in God's Providence, whatever sufferings He permits in our life can be turned into hope. We can inspire those around us by the way we accept our crosses and the hope that we have for Heaven.

We have such a relatively short time to influence people, and what are we using that time to do? Are we gossips? Are we justifying spiritual weakness? Do we indulge in vices together in social settings? How much wallowing in self-pity do we broadcast?

We can magnify the Lord in the world without being of the world, and this is how we should influence children or grandchildren, nieces, nephews, etc.… Are we openly inviting them to be saints? Do we use our own mortifications as an offering?

With foresight, we look forward, not backward. If our children are out of the house, we can't have regrets for how things were done in the past. We can only look at the example we give now and the way we can encounter our adult children or even our own parents if their faith life is struggling. What steps do we need to take to have the hard conversations about Jesus? What activities can we invite our family and friends to participate in to deepen their faith rather than their love of the world? And most of all, what prayers can we offer for our spiritual children?

Consider offering up your mortifications today for all children. Call them to a freer way of life by the standard of virtue you live out. How can you be warm and inviting, yet still holy, pure, and true? Prayerfully discern if God is asking you to be a part of someone's journey. Include "Come Alive (Dry Bones)" by Lauren Daigle if you'd like.

FORESIGHT & PROVIDENCE: DAY 77

Heaven is the goal; nothing on this earth can give us complete happiness. St. Thérèse is famous for writing, "the world is thy ship, not thy home," and she got that concept from her mother frequently quoting a poetic philosophic passage:

St. Zélie recited this to the Martin girls frequently: "Oh! Speak to me of the mysteries of this world that my desires foreshadow, into which my soul, weary of the shadows of the earth, aspires to immerse itself. Speak to me of the One who made it and fills it with himself and who alone can fill the immense void that he created in me."
– *Amschaspands et Darvands (Félicité Robert Lammenais, priest & philosopher)*

"True happiness is not in this world, and we are wasting time to look for it here."
– *St. Zélie Martin*

[speaking about pursuing sainthood] "I should have started sooner, while it was not so difficult; but in any case, 'better late than never.'" – *St. Zélie Martin*

St. Zélie's last written words: "God wants me to rest elsewhere than on earth"

Aren't we all full of desires? We all want to be loved, accepted, and affirmed. We all want to feel good and we want to be comfortable. No one, even the saints, desired suffering without first desiring the greatest Good. We can only desire a cross, or choose a voluntary mortification to offer up, if we have the foresight to see it is a means to the end goal of Heaven.

Life seems like drudgery when we don't look beyond ourselves. When we get stuck in a selfish mental pattern of greed and self-righteousness, we are constantly let down and unhappy because nothing will ever be enough. We were made for more, so letting material things be all we work for leaves us empty and angry. Living our life that way gives us a sense of bitterness that enslaves us. But seeking the transcendent happiness fills our souls with anticipation and hope; it gives us joy that can't be taken away and is a much better way to live. In fact, it's the life we were created for. God created us with an insatiable longing within our souls to know why we were created. Our life feels like it has purpose when we strive to know our Creator, to return His love with the best love we can give, and to live in true freedom. Freedom gives contentment in hope for life in our soul, whereas bitterness in insatiability gives destruction through death to our soul.

This is our Magnify 90 journey toward freedom. We are living to sharpen the virtues so that all of our worldly desires are rooted in pursuit of Heaven. Our worldview must be one that sees earth as a means to an end, with the foresight necessary to desire eternal happiness—not the finite pseudo-happiness offered by the world.

Consider

How have you been left wanting more from life? What makes you bitter? In what ways do you <u>not</u> live out the idea that the world is not your home? Have you been tempted to just give up Magnify 90? Are you looking for some sort of tangible reward? Are there any resolutions you can make to practice foresight regarding God's providential desires for your soul?

St. Zélie's letters can be seen in English in a variety of books; including Helene Mongin's The Extraordinary Parents of St. Thérèse of Lisieux: Sts. Louis and Zélie Martin translated by Marsha Daigle-Williamson (Our Sunday Visitor, 2015) and Celine Martin's The Mother of the Little Flower (TAN Books, 2005)

WEEKLY REFLECTIONS

Moderation

St. Gianna Molla

WEEK 12 - MODERATION
St. Gianna Molla

Mortifications	S	M	T	W	T	F	S
DAILY PRAYER (30 MIN) MAGNIFICAT, LITANY, ROSARY	✝	✝	✝	✝	✝	✝	✝
DAILY MASS							
CONFESSION (MONTHLY)							
ADORATION (WEEKLY)							
NO MAKEUP			✝		✝		
MEATLESS FASTING					✝		
INTENTIONAL WALK WITH FRIEND OR HUSBAND							
CONNECT WITH PERSON WHO CAME TO MIND IN PRAYER							
OTHER:							
OTHER:							
OTHER:							

Other Daily Mortifications to Remember

- ONLY CHRISTIAN/CLASSICAL MUSIC AND PODCASTS
- ONLY RELIGIOUS PROGRAMMING IN MODERATION
- NO WEIGHING ON A SCALE
- NO SWEETS, ALCOHOL, OR SNACKS IN BETWEEN MEALS
- NO SOCIAL MEDIA
- NO UNNECESSARY SHOPPING
- _____
- _____
- _____

I am offering my intentions for:

- S _____
- M _____
- T _____
- W _____
- T _____
- F _____
- S _____
- Other _____

Express Use this space to journal, draw, or otherwise express your thoughts on this week's virtue. Spend some time listening to the Holy Spirit, perhaps in Adoration, and capture whatever He brings to mind or lays on your heart.

MODERATION: DAY 78

Nearing the end of our intentional time spent in the "desert" of strict asceticism, let's reflect on temperance and how to find balance outside of something intentional like Magnify 90.

CCC 1809: *Temperance* is the moral virtue that moderates the attraction of pleasures and provides balance in the use of created goods. It ensures the will's mastery over instincts and keeps desires within the limits of what is honorable. The temperate person directs the sensitive appetites toward what is good and maintains a healthy discretion: "Do not follow your inclination and strength, walking according to the desires of your heart. (Sirach 5:2)" Temperance is often praised in the Old Testament: "Do not follow your base desires, but restrain your appetites. (Sirach 18:30) In the New Testament it is called "moderation" or "sobriety." We ought "to live sober, upright, and godly lives in this world. (Titus 2:12) "To live well is nothing other than to love God with all one's heart, with all one's soul and with all one's efforts; from this it comes about that love is kept whole and uncorrupted (through temperance). No misfortune can disturb it (and this is fortitude). It obeys only [God] (and this is justice), and is careful in discerning things, so as not to be surprised by deceit or trickery (and this is prudence). (St. Augustine)"

In our day to day life moving forward, we have to find a balance that promotes finding God in the goodness of earth but not losing Him amongst disordered desires. The virtue that helps us live out that balance and moderation is temperance. It is restraint against things we know don't help us become the saints we're meant to be.

We likely weren't perfect in our Magnify 90 mortifications; we likely indulged on some Sundays and solemnities—maybe we even forgot about something we had given up or we might have even just gone along with the crowd at a party. Hopefully we didn't just throw caution to the wind and completely misplace our sense of commitment. If this did happen, we can thank God for His mercy when we lose our way.

These 90 days should have shown us where our attachments truly lie by what we couldn't give up even for a few months. We have certain instincts that draw us to physical comforts and habits we have learned throughout our lives. These are the things we can really focus on using temperance with moving forward. Giving up dessert for the rest of our life is likely not necessary, nor is avoiding a snack —but there are certain habits we picked up or put down during Magnify that we need to keep up.

St. Augustine is quoted in the Catechism saying it is through temperance that we keep our love for God whole and uncorrupted. If we are able to make time to exercise 5 to 7 days a week, yet only make Mass a priority on Sundays…could we assess our schedule and motivation behind our commitments? Do we settle for giving God just 30 minutes a day, yet give ourselves an hour just to "get ready" for the day with hair and make-up routines? When we "veg out" watching two hours of TV a night but couldn't make time for a Rosary, again can we practice better temperance? Perhaps we can find a better balance between our spirituality and our bodily needs.

Remember, self-care is more than just relaxation; it is soul care. We must take care of our soul or we may end up losing it. Make a plan for maintaining virtuous growth, because if we stay stagnate, the devil will certainly swoop in with temptation and distraction that re-enslaves us.

Did you give into wine? Chocolate? Snacking? Online shopping? Why? What are you distracting yourself from? How can you seek balance with material/edible pleasures so that you are able to be social and celebratory, yet not attached such that these become "escapes" when prayer is the real solution? Can your Magnify 90 reflections help you form a personal rule of life, or fine-tune it if you already have one?

MODERATION: DAY 79

St. Gianna Molla, saint, wife, mother, doctor, feminine genius, is arguably the most balanced modern female saint.

Pietro Molla writing about his wife Gianna's heroic virtue; as part of the beatification process he wrote "to her" rather than in the third person: You knew how to accept and appreciate the Lord's gifts, the gifts of life without ever abusing them, without ever letting yourself be overcome. Your intentions and actions were completely consistent with your humility, with your sobriety. You gave me the example that life and nature, music and theater, mountains and trips, love and family can be enjoyed with temperance. For you the limits of temperance were clear: the limits of the law and of the grace of God. You know how to be disciplined; you preferred to serve than to be served. Yet in your temperance, your balance, your interior purity knew how to find room for full and perfect joy, for a message of serenity, of joy to all you approached. *(Pietro Molla. Saint Gianna Molla: Wife, Mother, Doctor* (2004) Ignatius Press)

"I was always told that the secret of happiness lay in living one moment at a time and in thanking the Lord for everything he sends us." – *St. Gianna*

For everything created by God is good, and nothing is to be rejected if it is received with thanksgiving; for then it is consecrated by the word of God and prayer.
– *1 Timothy 4:4-5*

St. Gianna knew how to enjoy the creation God gave us while still keeping His will at the forefront of her life. She wasn't attached in harmful ways to the joys and blessings of this life. St. Gianna's trusting love of God manifested in her way of being; everyone around her saw joy and beauty radiating from her soul as it moved from her interior peace to her active life. She tried to practice docility to the Lord's will in everything, and eventually it was that virtue of trust in Providence that led to her heroic declaration, "if you must decide between me and the child, do not hesitate, save the child—I insist on it. Save the baby." Her canonization was for more than just the pro-life statement when she had complications in pregnancy—her entire life had been one of virtue and love. Her canonization stands as a witness against the secularization and misguided "feminism" of the 1960s.

Baptized as Giovanna Francesca in 1922, St. Gianna was born into a large family, and two of her brothers became priests, with one in the beatification process—Servant of God Enrico Beretta. She wanted to join him as a missionary but was advised against it based on health. St. Gianna discerned her vocation to marriage, and pursued medicine as a career, because she knew it could pair well with family life given that she could set her own hours and bring Christ's love to other people she served. After 6 years of various encounters in passing through work, Pietro and Gianna had a ten-month courtship, then were married at 43 and 32. They had 4 children together. The pregnancies were especially hard on Gianna; the fourth ended in a C-section and complications that led to her death.

Frequent sacraments and trust in Divine Providence were key to her spirituality. She encountered God in others and especially in nature. She worked with Catholic Action, a group where she encouraged young girls to pursue a life lived for Christ. Her life was filled with more involuntary mortifications than voluntary ones—yet aren't these the ones that make us saints? The things we cannot change, because we didn't choose them, and don't have control over. Situations like illnesses, loss of loved ones, misunderstandings with others, separation from spouses due to work travel, uncertainty about the future—these were all offerings Gianna laid at the feet of Jesus.

How does your idea of temperance fits with Pietro's description of Gianna's. How is your whole life seen as a prayer? What connections do you personally see between a moderation, docility, and joy? On the flip side, how does rigidity and human perfectionism undermine holiness?

MODERATION: DAY 80

As we reflected on last week, our trust in God's Providence helps us utilize prudence. We can discern what community around us we need to help maintain a balanced life.

Be sober, be watchful. Your adversary the devil prowls around like a roaring lion, seeking someone to devour. Resist him, firm in your faith, knowing that the same experience of suffering is required of your brotherhood throughout the world. And after you have suffered a little while, the God of all grace, who has called you to his eternal glory in Christ, will himself restore, establish, and strengthen you.
– *1 Peter 5:8-10*

"We must act, we must enter into all the fields of social, familiar and political action. And to work, because all the dark and threatening forces of evil are united. It is necessary that the forces of good be all united and form a kind of dam, a barrier as if to say: 'There is no passing over here.'" – *St. Gianna*

Growing in the virtue of moderation helps us fight the temptation to give into our sensual vices completely in moments of weakness or social pressure. Temptation comes from the Latin *temptare* meaning "to handle, to test, to try out." Temptation says, "try this out, it'll make you happy," or "you can handle this on your own; you're strong enough to keep it from being sinful," or "give this a try; it'll fill that longing." Temptation for humans started with Satan telling Eve all those things…and here we are today, still battling the same devil. These days it also sounds like, "You've already sinned today, just give into ___ since you're off the wagon anyways." "You can't trust anyone; fill the loneliness with things instead." One sin does not mean we need to sin again. To seek freedom from slavery to sin, a life of moderation helps us to rightly order tangible things and activities. Balance is necessary for the active life.

In our desire for fulfillment, happiness, or approval, the devil tempts us. Satan is out to "devour" a soul like a lion. Constantly being around people that draw us into worldly attachments isn't prudent or helpful. We need a community that holds us accountable, inspires us to greatness, and helps us grow in holiness necessary for this life on earth. So we seek to fellowship with other Christians, knowing they are fighting the same battle. We also call upon angels for assistance. God's helpers will sustain us as we go out into the world magnifying Him while resisting sin, because while the community that strengthens us is necessary, we can't remain there constantly. We are called to go out—to be mission minded people.

It's important to note, just because we can "moderate" our consumption of created things doesn't mean our intention is always pure. Our motivation for just one drink likely turns sinful when we claim we "need" it to calm our nerves so we can feel relaxed. Wanting to just sit down to check social media before bed goes wrong when we use it to fulfill our desire for intimacy, yet we distance ourselves from our husbands. Our temptation to daily indulge a constant sweet tooth leads to an open door to even more cravings that impede our health and mental stability.

Perhaps in the name of being a "good" mom, we place our children's extracurricular and sport involvements above our commitment to activities for spiritual growth…and what does that witness say to them? Maybe we hear a bit of gossip and think it won't be too bad if we indulge a bit before bowing out of the conversation when it gets really bad.

A clarification that wine, social media, dessert, sports, and unwinding with friends are not sinful! We must use temperance to help us check our motivations behind these and other things. Life beyond Magnify 90 is finding a balance and the right intention for things of the world. If we sincerely pray before we work and play, then our temperance should be able to help us have the right balance in life.

Are you on guard against spiritual attacks? Where are your weaknesses? Does temptation usually strike at a certain time of day, week, or month? Does being around certain people lead you into more temptation? How do you live in the world, enjoying it, but keeping your heart guarded from sin? How much do you want to be a saint? Enough that it makes you try to avoid even venial sin?

MODERATION: DAY 81

Magnifying the Lord means we are reflecting His light unto the whole world and we can't keep it hidden. We've been given a great grace through detaching from worldly things but we know we can't sustain a holy life alone.

No one after lighting a lamp puts it in a cellar or under a bushel, but on a stand, that those who enter may see the light. Your eye is the lamp of your body; when your eye is sound, your whole body is full of light; but when it is not sound, your body is full of darkness. Therefore be careful lest the light in you be darkness. If then your whole body is full of light, having no part dark, it will be wholly bright, as when a lamp with its rays gives you light. – *Luke 11:33-36*

"Lord, may this light you have lit in my soul never be extinguished." – *St. Gianna*

"Our body is a cenacle, a monstrance: through its crystal the world should see God." – *St. Gianna*

CCC 1810: Human virtues acquired by education, by deliberate acts and by a perseverance ever-renewed in repeated efforts are purified and elevated by divine grace. With God's help, they forge character and give facility in the practice of the good. The virtuous [wo]man is happy to practice them.

Scripture tells us that when we are full of light, full of virtue, we shouldn't try to hide it. We are to persevere in God's mission for us—growing ever closer to Him and bringing others along the way too. We evangelize through our life; through the activities we participate in and things we speak about. We don't let the culture change us; we live changing the culture around us.

We have spent these past few months learning, growing, and practicing the kind of life holy women are called to lead—lives that aren't attached to vices. We've made intentional choices to try again, and we've gotten back up through mercy when we've fallen. The graces we've received may never be made known to us personally, but we can rest assured that God has extended His Divine help, so we move forward transformed. We should never turn our back to the lessons we've learned since day one; just because Magnify 90 is winding down doesn't mean we stop growing in virtue to magnify the Lord!

It's prudent to formulate a plan for handling those temptations that might extinguish Christ's light in us. We don't want to run out of Magnify 90 ready to throw all the options for recreation and comfort back on the table. We may likely over-do it and have a sort of "rebound phase". We must be prepared with that knowledge. To keep our joy and peace, we've got to daily choose virtue over vice—choosing to indulge only in things that remind us of God's beauty through all our senses. Like St. Gianna indicates, our very bodies and souls are created to reveal a piece of God's glory, so everything we take in should magnify Him.

Consider

Have you thought about ways in which you've grown during Magnify 90? What struggles do you still have? Do you ever pull back or try to hide your love of God? How do you struggle to avoid letting the flame flicker? Is there someone in your life you've given up sharing the Gospel with? Can you keep the light exposed for them? Is there someone in your life that needs the witness of a temperate life?

MODERATION: DAY 82

We may be tempted to return to the lifestyle we had before Magnify 90, but striving to keep our soul totally connected to God will keep our life in balance.

"Jesus would say to us: What is a person? A person is not only body. In that body there is thought, a will, which is capable of meeting suffering, which could not happen otherwise. In the body there is a spirit, and as such it is immortal. There is an abyss between body and soul; they are two very different entities, but they are united. What would Jesus say to you? You should take care of this body. God has so inserted the divine in the human that everything we do assumes greater value." – *St. Gianna (*Pietro Molla. *Saint Gianna Molla: Wife, Mother, Doctor* (2004) Ignatius Press)

"…The world seeks joy but does not find it because it is far from God. We, full of the joy that comes from Jesus, carry joy in our hearts with Jesus. He will be the strength that helps us." – *St. Gianna*

No temptation has overtaken you that is not common to man. God is faithful, and he will not let you be tempted beyond your strength, but with the temptation will also provide the way of escape, that you may be able to endure it. – *1 Corinthians 10: 13*

Recognizing the unity of our body and soul gives us an insight that lifts our actions to a level beyond a secular appetite for control. Everything we do is for His Glory in the world. Our virtues begin in our soul's disposition, but they affect our active life—the one others see. The active life takes place through the body, in the world, and it must be balanced because we know the world isn't our final destination. Our souls, however, do not need to be "balanced"; they must be entirely reverent, completely pure, and totally docile toward God. A soul fully alive in God will seek Him in all that the body does. We want to be saints? There's no place for balance in our souls, and the more we direct our soul to God, the better we practice moderation in the world. Working in a garden? Make sure it brings glory to God. Going on a vacation? Make sure it brings God glory. Going to the gym? Make sure it brings God glory. Having friends over for dinner? Sending a message? Leading a class field trip? Writing a book? Listening to music? Stuck at the office? Spreading the gospel? Playing a sport or game? Going shopping or to a party? Bring God glory, not yourself or another human. Find ways to always bring it back to Him.

We must eat, but not make it a god. We must sleep, but not make it a god. We must work, but not make it a god. We must recreate and play, but not make it a god. We must be free, but it cannot become an idol affecting our pride if we seek sinful "freedom from God". By keeping God always present in the front of our minds, we can avoid sin easier, stay joyful, and shine His light into the world.

Our interior life is where God's strength is revealed even when our active life seems impossible. No doubt some of us are fighting illness, are exhausted from a new child, or are struggling to care for loved ones. Maybe we battle anxiety and mental illness.

These things can all bring God glory when we trust in His strength and His goodness and persevere in our Christian life. (Read CCC 1532 and surrounding passages about the Anointing of the Sick for more on this.) Overcoming temptation to despair because life seems hard requires a soul that is not balanced; we must **fully** trust God, **fully** hope in Him, and **fully** love Him.

What part of your soul are you still trying to hide from God— what piece of your life do you try to fill with worldly goods? How does your balanced active life reflect the state of your soul as it should be fully committed to God?

MODERATION: DAY 83

St. Therese of Lisieux wrote, "The nearer one gets to God, the simpler one becomes." We must root out our sneaky sins that can get glossed over by saying we are "good enough."

What causes wars, and what causes fightings among you? Is it not your passions that are at war in your members? You desire and do not have; so you kill. And you covet and cannot obtain; so you fight and wage war. You do not have, because you do not ask. You ask and do not receive, because you ask wrongly, to spend it on your passions. Unfaithful creatures! Do you not know that friendship with the world is enmity with God? Therefore whoever wishes to be a friend of the world makes himself an enemy of God. – *James 4:1-4*

CCC 1811: It is not easy for man, wounded by sin, to maintain moral balance. Christ's gift of salvation offers us the grace necessary to persevere in the pursuit of the virtues. Everyone should always ask for this grace of light and strength, frequent the sacraments, cooperate with the Holy Spirit, and follow his calls to love what is good and shun evil.

"Christian life is not achieved by people who do little, but by those who commit themselves completely." – *St. Gianna*

We can see the hurt and loneliness that causes so much of the despair in the world. There's such a lack of moderation. People are over-consuming everything in hopes of feeling satisfied, but all they feel is empty. They ask for all the wrong things, the things that become idols, rather than asking for things that point their souls to an eternity with God. We find excellence in our spiritual life when we come to sense the right way to live in the world but not be a lover of it. As we become simpler in our lives, detached from worldly things and actions, we can see the need for a fully committed relationship with God more clearly. When we recognize our pride and selfish tendencies as we pray the Litany of Humility, it still stings. That's good because it means we are taking it to heart.

Our simplicity can help reveal our sophisticated sins that easily slide under the radar. We aren't often committing mortal sins such as adultery, stealing, or intentionally missing Mass. It's the little sin of being uncharitable in uncomfortable circumstances, or being cold-shouldered to the person that rubs us the wrong way, or telling God "not yet…in a little while," or wanting to add our opinions to the conversation first and loudest, or avoiding a healthy conflict because it takes effort to be calm and virtuous in the heat of it. The virtue of moderation is sometimes about acknowledging the things we should have but didn't do when we were doing the things we shouldn't have done.

Working on temperance reveals where we need to moderate the attachments to food, drink, intimacy, and entertainment. Let us pray that what remains at the end of these 90 days reveals ways in which we still aren't fully committed to being like Saints, so that we can ask God for the grace of light and strength to persevere in virtue!

Consider How is moderation related to magnanimity? Have you ever considered what the least amount of commitment you can have is? Have you looked at Mass as an obligation and not a gift? What areas of your life do you need to stop asking "What's the minimum?" and ask, "What brings God the most glory through my way of living?"

MODERATION: DAY 84

God has given us grace through Jesus Christ and the Holy Spirit; it is our choice to be open to bearing "new fruit" and choosing life each day.

"Lord, keep your grace in my heart. Live in me so that Your grace may be mine. Make it that I may bear everyday some flowers and new fruit." – *St. Gianna*

But the word is very near you; it is in your mouth and in your heart, so that you can do it. See, I have set before you this day life and good, death and evil. If you obey the commandments of the Lord your God which I command you this day, by loving the Lord your God, by walking in his ways, and by keeping his commandments and his statutes and his ordinances, then you shall live and multiply, and the Lord your God will bless you in the land which you are entering to take possession of it. But if your heart turns away, and you will not hear, but are drawn away to worship other gods and serve them, I declare to you this day, that you shall perish; you shall not live long in the land which you are going over the Jordan to enter and possess. I call heaven and earth to witness against you this day, that I have set before you life and death, blessing and curse; therefore choose life that you and your descendants may live… – *Deuteronomy 30:14-19*

Just because we have accepted God's grace, mercy, and forgiveness does not take away our concupiscence. Do we dare think that God is done with us? We must wake up each day and choose to live by loving the Lord with all our heart and soul. We renew our fidelity to God as the center of our lives each day. This is possible with the Word of God, Jesus Christ, in the Eucharist through the gift of the Holy Spirit guiding the Church. Whether we make it to daily Mass or not, we can keep a daily appointment with the Lord in prayer and unite our daily life to the sacrifice of the Mass through the Morning Offering.

We have been blessed with the one, true, apostolic Church. Why do we go to Mass? Why do we have the sacraments?

- *To bring God glory and praise and honor.* The sacrifice of the Mass isn't about us; it's about what we owe God for His mercy, which we aren't actually able to repay in our fallen nature. This is why we humbly offer God *Himself* like He taught us at the last supper. Our participation at Mass is an offering of humility and love—and it is an assent to Christ's offering. Regardless of what we "take away" from a homily or "get out" of the music, we are transformed by receiving God into our very being. We are transformed from the inside out through our openness to grace.

- *To receive the grace necessary for daily living.* Are we living out gratitude for access to Eucharist and confession? Do we frequently run toward the Lord's true presence? St. Gianna made daily Mass a priority, even when she was on vacation because she knew it gave her the strength necessary to live a balanced life in the world.

She knew it helped her to be a woman of virtue, to bear fruit. We keep balance in our daily life best through consuming our true Daily Bread. We must not receive Our Lord and then go about our life like we didn't just experience a miracle. Each experience at Mass should be treated as a foretaste of eternal life as we remember the choirs of angels and the communion of Saints are present there praising God!

Can you prepare for Mass and Holy Communion better? How do you shape your entire life around the Source and Summit (that is, the Eucharist) of your faith? Have you ever considered your life outside Mass as preparation for the next Mass and Mass as preparation for your life beyond it?

WEEKLY REFLECTIONS

Perseverance & Way of the Cross

St. Mary Magdalene

WEEK 13 - PERSEVERANCE & WAY OF THE CROSS
St. Mary Magdalene

Mortifications	S	M	T	W	T	F	S
DAILY PRAYER (30 MIN) MAGNIFICAT, LITANY, ROSARY	✝	✝	✝	✝	✝	✝	✝
DAILY MASS							
CONFESSION (MONTHLY)							
ADORATION (WEEKLY)							
NO MAKEUP			✝			✝	
MEATLESS FASTING						✝	
INTENTIONAL WALK WITH FRIEND OR HUSBAND							
CONNECT WITH PERSON WHO CAME TO MIND IN PRAYER							
OTHER:							
OTHER:							
OTHER:							

Other Daily Mortifications to Remember

- ONLY CHRISTIAN/CLASSICAL MUSIC AND PODCASTS
- ONLY RELIGIOUS PROGRAMMING IN MODERATION
- NO WEIGHING ON A SCALE
- NO SWEETS, ALCOHOL, OR SNACKS IN BETWEEN MEALS
- NO SOCIAL MEDIA
- NO UNNECESSARY SHOPPING
- _____
- _____
- _____

I am offering my intentions for:

S ● _____
M ● _____
T ● _____
W ● _____
T ● _____
F ● _____
S ● _____
Other ● _____

Express

Use this space to journal, draw, or otherwise express your thoughts on this week's virtue. Spend some time listening to the Holy Spirit, perhaps in Adoration, and capture whatever He brings to mind or lays on your heart.

PERSEVERANCE & WAY OF THE CROSS: DAY 85

Our growth in virtue and removing worldly attachments has prepared us to journey with Christ as we are called to pick up our crosses and follow Him. We effectively witness the Gospel when we joyfully give God exaltation through our hardships. In these closing days of Magnify 90, reflect on the Way of the Cross with the feminine genius of Mary Magdalene.

Every Christian relives the experience of Mary Magdalene. It involves an encounter which changes our lives: the encounter with a unique Man who lets us experience all God's goodness and truth, Who frees us from evil not in a superficial and fleeting way, but sets us free radically, heals us completely and restores our dignity. This is why Mary Magdalene calls Jesus "my hope": He was the one who allowed her to be reborn, who gave her a new future, a life of goodness and freedom from evil. "Christ my hope" means that all my yearnings for goodness find in Him a real possibility of fulfilment: with Him I can hope for a life that is good, full and eternal, for God himself has drawn near to us, even sharing our humanity.
– *Pope Benedict XVI (Easter 2012)*

"My beloved daughter, in order to sustain thee, I give thee, Mary Magdalen for mother; thou canst address thyself to her in all assurance, I charge her with you in a special manner." – *Our Lord to St. Catherine of Siena* (Raymond of Capua. *Life of St. Catharine* (1860) PF Cunningham)

Redemptive suffering is a choice; we can use it to magnify the Lord. Suffering comes from Latin meaning "bear under" or to "carry up," which is to say, endure. When we endure a burden, we join in Christ's redemptive work. Jesus truly came to encounter humans and draw them up toward the Father. Visually, imagine a hand reaching down and a hand reaching up. Let us always reach up with openness, never close in on ourselves.

When we intentionally stay close to God despite enduring pain, embarrassment, loneliness, or illness, we acknowledge that God doesn't give us a cross to hurt us. Trials come our way because He loves us so much that free will was given to us. Jesus suffered for us to be reconciled to the Father; so too are we called to accept suffering out of imitation of Christ.

Meditating on the agony in the garden, we recall how important Adoration and thanksgiving after Holy Communion are in sustaining our faith life. We can't let these two sources of grace instituted by Christ on Holy Thursday become another box to check off as done for the week. *Can't we stay to pray with Him?* Let us not rush off after Holy Communion or depart quickly after Mass.

Mary Magdalene has been given the title of Prophetess of Eucharistic Love and Apostle to the Apostles. She shows us what it's like to sin, be forgiven, and then stay near to the Source of Mercy. She worshiped Christ at His feet, walked near Him along the Way of the Cross, loved Him at the foot of the cross, and came to His tomb as soon as the Sabbath was over to adore Him there as well. Her spirituality of never leaving Jesus should be ours as well. When we physically must depart from His Presence, we can carry Him with us deep in our soul and prominently in our mind.

Consider When can you dwell in the house of the Lord a little while longer? Is there anywhere more significant to be than His presence? Reflect on ways you've made yourself the center of your own universe, and resolve to keep God at the center of all you do, not just another spinning planet revolving around you. If you'd like, add "Death in His Grave" by John Mark McMillan as the week meditating on the Way of the Cross begins.

PERSEVERANCE & WAY OF THE CROSS: DAY 86

We need God's mercy to have Eternal Life, and while His mercy is free—we can't be so full of other things that there's no place in our soul for it to fill. Pride and envy will be our downfall if we do not practice virtue as we follow along the way of Christ's cross.

The governor again said to them, "Which of the two do you want me to release for you?" And they said, "Barabbas." Pilate said to them, "Then what shall I do with Jesus who is called Christ?" They all said, "Let him be crucified." And he said, "Why, what evil has he done?" But they shouted all the more, "Let him be crucified." So when Pilate saw that he was gaining nothing, but rather that a riot was beginning, he took water and washed his hands before the crowd, saying, "I am innocent of this righteous man's blood; see to it yourselves." – *Matthew 27: 21-24*

"Most of all I imitate the conduct of the Magdalene, astonishing or rather her loving audacity which charms the Heart of Jesus also attracts my own. Yes, I feel it; even though I had on my conscience all the sins that can be committed, I would go, my heart broken with sorrow, and throw myself into Jesus' arms, for I know how much He loves the prodigal child who returns to Him." – *St. Therese of Lisieux* (St. Therese of Lisieux. *Story of a Soul: Study Edition,* translator Marc Foley OCD, (2005) ICS Publications)

The Stations of the Cross most frequently begin with Jesus being condemned to die. There's an irony on how justice and mercy intertwine with the Way of the Cross. We see that Jesus was condemned to die by a disregard for justice—Pilate didn't want to deal with the backlash over the fact that he couldn't find any guilt in Jesus, so he didn't save Jesus despite having the chance. Conversely, we are condemned to die for our sins because of justice, but are saved through a deeper mercy. We don't deserve to have life everlasting, but the offering of Christ's innocence turned "guilt" is what gives us the hope for eternity spent with God. We must be changed by the visible sign of God's love: the cross. We can't be ignorant of His sacrifice nor of His mercy.

Next along the way, we come to the point where Jesus takes up His Cross. We are called to imitate Him in how we take up our crosses and don't run away from them. In our modern world, we could do many things to hide from suffering, but we must be sober, alert, and present. We must persevere through hardships—yes, we use prudence regarding health and safety—but we face them bravely and open to the ways in which Christ wants to refine our souls.

Like Mary Magdalene we follow Christ along the Way of the Cross because of how much He loves us, how much He forgives us—and what response that deserves from us.

We've reflected frequently on involuntary suffering and also asceticism so that by these crosses we walk with Jesus. We know that without virtuously enduring the trials of this life, we cannot have much hope for our own salvation. We unite our sufferings to His sacrifice as a co-redemptive offering of mercy. Perseverance is a virtue necessary to walk the Way of the Cross.

Consider

In a meditation about the first station, just before becoming Pope Benedict XVI, Cardinal Joseph Ratzinger wrote,

The quiet voice of conscience is drowned out by the cries of the crowd. Evil draws its power from indecision and concern for what other people think.

How indecisive are you regarding ways to take a stand against injustice, specifically toward God? Do you suppress your conscience by any means so that sin slips into your life frequently? Are you attached to not rocking the boat? Can you work to change this?

PERSEVERANCE & WAY OF THE CROSS: DAY 87

From Sacred Tradition we hear of Jesus falling three times along the way to Golgotha. How heavy our sins weigh upon Him.

Surely he has borne our griefs and carried our sorrows; yet we esteemed him stricken smitten by God and afflicted. But he was wounded for our transgressions, he was bruised for our iniquities; upon him was the chastisement that made us whole, and with his bruises we are healed. All we like sheep have gone astray; we have turned everyone to his own way; and the Lord has laid on him the iniquity of us all. – *Isaiah 53:4-6*

The story of Mary of Magdala reminds us all of a fundamental truth: a disciple of Christ is one who, in the experience of human weakness, has had the humility to ask for his help, has been healed by Him and has set out following closely after Him, becoming a witness of the power of His merciful love that is stronger than sin and death. – *Pope Benedict XVI (July 23, 2006)*

How frequently we try to run away from things that could make us saints. Out of pride we think we know better. We try to face the hardships in life on our own and end up falling under the weight of our sin. Distractions weaken our resolve and fear of losing control hinders our steps.

Jesus knows what weight of sin feels like, not from His own of course, but from bearing ours. He doesn't want us to struggle under the cross alone—He wants to make our burden feel lighter by sharing in it. He asks us to seek mercy. We ask for help, just like Mary Magdalene did in the gospel. Watching Him carry the cross, Mary Magdalene was aware of her past sins, but did she still feel the weight of them as she watched the Lord fall? Why didn't she run away like the other apostles? Perhaps it was because she knew the Good Shepherd's voice. Perhaps it was because she didn't have any arrogance left in her soul. Was it especially because Christ's mother was there, inspiring her continued love in Jesus?

Mary Magdalene certainly accompanied the Blessed Mother many times before, as a woman among the followers of Christ. She learned virtue, love, and contemplation from His mother. The pair went along the Way of the Cross, horrified but ever faithful and ever loving. We have much to learn from the witness of Mary Magdalene staying even closer to Mary, who brings us intimately closer to Jesus's love.

Consider Read Lamentations 3 today. It reminds us that we will certainly face things that seem too hard to bear, but God's steadfast love is forever. Why do you keep hope alive in the cross? How do you live as a witness that love is stronger than death?

Two separate stations along the Way of the Cross can be meditated upon together: Jesus meeting His mother Mary, and Jesus encountering the weeping women. St. Therese said, "We must forget ourselves, and put aside our tastes and ideas, and guide souls not by our own way, but along the path which Our Lord points out."

As the Mother of Mercy, she bends over her children who still face dangers and exhaustion, to see their sufferings, to hear the cry arising from their afflictions, to bring them comfort and to renew their hope of peace. – *Pope St. John Paul II (2003)*

Jesus turning to them said, "Daughters of Jerusalem, do not weep for me, but weep for yourselves and for your children. For behold, the days are coming when they will say, 'Blessed are the barren, and the wombs that never bore, and the breasts that never gave suck!' Then they will begin to say to the mountains, 'Fall on us'; and to the hills, 'Cover us'. For if they do this when the wood is green, what will happen when it is dry? – *Luke 23:28-31*

While there is no Scripture passage that tells us Jesus met His mother along the Way of the Cross, Sacred Tradition tells us He did. Because of the deep love Jesus has for Mary, His mother, we can believe that He would have consoled her. For Mary, the Way of the Cross culminated with Christ's declaration as her Mother to us all. Her pierced heart is united to His pierced side in agape love as a tender gift to humanity. She shows us to bring our wounds to His wounds where His Blood redeems us and we find hope for salvation.

Mother Mary is the perfect example for us all, but perhaps we find it hard to imitate her. We may use the excuse that she doesn't seem approachable because she is immaculate. This is the devil tempting us, because he knows how powerful she is! When we find it too difficult to model our life upon Mary our Mother, let us go to her through Mary Magdalene. She was not perfect, so in her we can easily see ourselves—sinners turned apostles. And she didn't leave the side of Mother Mary, even when the road got hard, so neither should we. These two women show us what God really wants along the Way of the Cross—closeness and fidelity, striving for perfect love in our relationships.

When Jesus told the women of Jerusalem not to weep for Him, but for themselves and future generations, it was an instruction to take our sins seriously. The women represent the Church as a whole, and Jesus showed that not everyone goes to heaven. Over 2000 years since Christ, we can assume that wood is dry now. How are we living? For what do we weep? Do we weep over offenses against the dignity of humans, against the beauty of marriage and the priesthood, against irreverent or absent worship of God?

Consider

How has praying the Rosary affected your perseverance in the Way of the Cross? How do you seek consolation from Jesus? When has He consoled you in a manner you weren't expecting? Do you seek to encounter Christ daily? Add "When Love Sees You" by Mac Powell to your prayer today if you'd like. Consider the book *Mary Magdalene: Prophetess of Eucharistic Love* by Fr. Sean Davidson (Ignatius Press, 2017) as a way to grow further in the feminine genius seen in Mary Magdalene.

We can meditate upon Simon carrying the cross together with Veronica wiping the face of Jesus because both show us ways to console Jesus in our equal dignity.

And as they led him away, they seized one Simon of Cyrene, who was coming in from the country, and laid on him the cross, to carry it behind Jesus. *– Luke 23:26*

Indeed, the Evil One always seeks to spoil God's work, sowing division in the human heart, between body and soul, between the individual and God, in interpersonal, social and international relations, as well as between human beings and creation. The Evil One sows discord; God creates peace. [...] Surely goodness and mercy shall follow me all the days of my life; and I shall dwell in the house of the Lord forever" (Psalm 23:6) Dear friends, these words make our heart beat fast for they express our deepest desire, they say what we are made for: life, eternal life! These are the words of those who, like Mary Magdalene, have experienced God in their life and know His peace. *– Pope Benedict XVI (July 22, 2012)*

In the face of freedom to sin, we must ask ourselves, "How do I become a saint—what is *God's* will for me?" This is the path to holiness. We use our freedom to serve others, not ourselves, because it is in this very servant-hearted nature that we ourselves *can be saved*. This is the witness of Christ and this is the example of Simon and Veronica. These two stations of the cross can show us that God intends men and women to work together, not in competition, nor in resentment, for the glory of God. Men and women are each called to imitate Christ's sacrificial love through a complementary nature. Veronica cared for Jesus in His loneliness and aching, exhausted body along the way. Simon carried the sheer weight of Christ's unjust condemnation by accepting a cross that was not his own.

Why did Sacred Tradition preserve meditating upon the station of Veronica wiping the face of Christ? This beautiful testament to the vocation of women as consoling Christ serves as a reminder that we bear Christ's image—we magnify Him to the world! Women's receptive genius gives foundation to our spirituality. We reveal the human longing to receive God. Just as Veronica supported Christ along the Way of the Cross, so too are we called to help fortify the virtues of others by our own feminine genius.

Simon carrying the cross is like fatherhood, whether spiritual or physical. Jesus shows the way and then men take up behind Him—in marriage, the priesthood, or celibate consecrated life. Men must be spiritual leaders if nature is to be as God intended. Do we as women support men in their call from God or do we fight over whether it should be ours too? None of us, men or women, are our own—we leave behind our desires to freely choose God's will.

As women seeking to magnify the Lord, we are to be the conduits of light and life. Our dignity is heightened by preserving the dignity of all persons. How frequently it seems in today's age, whether it is out of envy or pride, women try to keep every option within their grasp, often choking out the dignity of men. Our path to sanctification will never trample over others, woman or men.

Consider

How do you look to Mary, Mary Magdalene, Veronica, and all the feminine genius saints we've meditated with during our Magnify 90 as exemplars of the dignity of women in the Church? What does being a foundation for the spirituality of others look like to you? What is your understanding of women's complementary nature with men?

If you're unsure, do some further reading on the topic; being well-versed in this topic is necessary to encourage the genius of women at large. A great starting point is St. John Paul II, *Man & Woman He Created Them -Theology of the Body* (2006) Pauline Books & Media. If that is a daunting book to begin, there are several books for beginners that break it down, and a Theology of the Body study.

PERSEVERANCE & WAY OF THE CROSS: DAY 90

Jesus is stripped of his garments, nailed to the cross, and dies. He is laid in His mother's arms. Her faith is not passive and ours cannot be either. Our fiat, like Mary's, will always involve contemplation and action. As we meditate along the Way of the Cross, we see ways to serve the Body of Christ.

"Truly, truly, I say to you, unless a grain of wheat falls into the earth and dies, it remains alone; but if it dies, it bears much fruit. He who loves his life loses it, and he who hates his life in this world will keep it for eternal life. If any one serves me, he must follow me; and where I am, there shall my servant be also; if any one serves me, the Father will honor him. [...] and I, when I am lifted up from the earth, will draw all men to myself." – *John 12:24-26, 32*

"If you have the courage to imitate Mary Magdalene in her sins, have the courage to imitate her penance!" – *St. Padre Pio*

In the stripping of His garments, the nature of Christ's humanity is expressed in humiliation, pain, and suffering. As the "New Adam," Christ was exposed despite His sinlessness—whereas Adam had concealed himself after his sin. In our journey along the Way of the Cross, we are also called to lay down our coverups. We seek to be purified from the inside out by laying aside our attachments.

Next, as Jesus is nailed to the cross, He and the Father are one. Their saving work is a message to us —*I love you. I suffer for you.* God did not create the world and then just leave it spinning—uninvolved and unconcerned. The very presence of Jesus upon the earth is proof that we were created to be with Him. He desires relationship with us. He gave us the Church, and the Holy Spirit guides us even now. We aren't left wandering or wondering.

Mary Magdalene knew the love of Christ's sweetness and pure joy, so she sought to stay always near to Christ so that she could have the *opportunity* to love Him and be loved by Him. What a great model for us. Her "penance," referenced by Padre Pio for the sins of her past was lingering at the foot of the cross, adoring His bruised figure, covered with the very Precious Blood that saves. Following this example, we seek to dwell in the *blood and water* that pour forth from His side as we approach the sacramental grace and mercy offered to us in the Church.

When Christ died on the cross, He showed us infinite mercy. We are incapable of showing God mercy because we are imperfect; we can't give perfect love. But paradoxically we can't go to Heaven without perfect love. This is the mystery of redemption and salvation. Christ's death and resurrection gave us redemption; it paid the price. Salvation comes from our response to that loving act.

When Christ was laid in His mother's arms, we see unity between Christ's sacrificed body and the Body, the Church, held by our Blessed Mother. Holding this image in our mind, we see our hope for Heaven. It is why we want to magnify the Lord—to love Him in others because it's impossible to love Him enough.

Think of the gravitational pull of the world scientifically "caused" Christ's death upon the cross. It compounded with the pain of crucifixion to literally suffocate Him. Does the world ever suffocate you? Where do you catch your breath? When do you feel closest to Christ? How have you tried to love God in the past? How can you love Him deeper at the foot of the cross?

PERSEVERANCE & WAY OF THE CROSS: DAY 91

We've spent so long in the desert, we may be exhausted, parched, and empty. This is where God calls us to rise to new life, transformed. Moving forward, we have habits and knowledge of saints, Scripture, and virtues to keep us growing into the holy women God wants of us.

And you shall know that I am the Lord, when I open your graves, and raise you from your graves, O my people. And I will put my Spirit within you, and you shall live and I will place you in your own land… – *Ezekiel 37:13-14*

When I come to a human heart in Holy Communion," He said, "My hands are full of all kinds of graces which I want to give to the soul. But souls do not even pay attention to Me; they leave Me to Myself and busy themselves with other things. [...] They treat Me as a dead object" – *(No. 1385, Diary of Saint Maria Faustina Kowalska (1987) Marian Fathers)*

The ancient liturgical Sequence addresses Mary Magdalen because it was granted to her not only to discover the tomb empty but also to announce the event to the Apostles. Peter and John ran to the tomb and found that what the women were saying was true. / Rejoice, Mary of Magdala! Rejoice, Peter and John! Rejoice, Apostles one and all! Rejoice, o Church, for the tomb is empty. Christ is risen! Where they had placed him there are only the linen cloths and the shroud in which they had wrapped him on Good Friday. Proclaim with us and with the whole of humanity: "Surrexit Christus spes mea - Surrexit Christus spes nostra!" – *Pope Saint John Paul II (Easter 1997)*

The final station of the cross: Jesus is laid in the tomb. Those assembled at His burial included only one Apostle, yet it included many women and lay men. This shows us love through the feminine genius and Christ's desire to sanctify the whole world. Attendants to Christ in His weakest moments, women are crucial to the ministry of the Body of Christ, especially where Christ suffers in the poor, the marginalized, and the sick. As others struggle under the weight of their crosses, women are especially called to light the way to Christ's love.

When the Sabbath was over, Mary Magdalene ran to the tomb. Not seeing Jesus anywhere, she was scared because she didn't know where He was. Fear, when it's healthy, indicates we care about something. She was scared because she cared for Jesus. She didn't have the knowledge like we do now; it wasn't until He greeted Her and sent her on her mission, that she knew there was no reason to fear. Jesus Christ had risen as He said! She ran to magnify the Lord to the others as apostle to the apostles.

We should never be scared into despair, so long as we know that Jesus Christ is not dead—He is alive! We have the True Presence of Jesus in Communion as the source and summit of our faith. We must be witnesses in our parishes to never treat Him in the manner He described to St. Faustina. The Way of the Cross shows us what to do with our growth in devotion and virtue. We die to ourselves and step out of the tomb of fear, which in a sense, is the basis of all sinful attachments. We run unto the world and proclaim the Good News!

Consider

Reflect on what your life looked like when you began Magnify 90. How has it changed? What are your intentions moving forward now? Will you keep up any mortifications or devotions on a regular basis? How will you handle involuntary mortifications with joy? How are you called to specifically magnify the Lord in the sphere of influence around you?

WEEKLY REFLECTIONS

FINAL REFLECTIONS

What is the biggest change or shift I recognize in my life as a result of Magnify 90?

_____

_____

_____

_____

_____

_____

_____

_____

What was hardest for me?

_____

_____

_____

_____

_____

_____

_____

_____

What am I most grateful for from this past 90 days?

_____

_____

_____

_____

_____

_____

_____

_____

What prayer intentions did I see answered or consolations did I receive during Magnify 90?

_____

_____

_____

_____

_____

_____

_____

_____

What mortifications or devotions do I intend to keep ongoing in my life?

_____

_____

_____

_____

_____

_____

_____

_____

Consider coming back to this space on a monthly basis, perhaps as part of a First Friday or First Saturday Devotion, and reflect on lasting impacts from Magnify 90 that you continue to recognize in your life at that time. Also consider the things that have fallen to the wayside in your practice of faith that perhaps you'd like to rekindle or strengthen.

Date: _____

_____

_____

_____

_____

_____

_____

Date: _____

_____

_____

_____

_____

_____

_____

Date: _____

_____

_____

_____

_____

_____

_____

Date:

_____

_____

_____

_____

_____

_____

_____

Date:

_____

_____

_____

_____

_____

_____

_____

Date:

_____

_____

_____

_____

_____

_____

_____

Date:

_____

_____

_____

_____

_____

_____

Date:

_____

_____

_____

_____

_____

_____

Date:

_____

_____

_____

_____

_____

_____

MAGNIFICAT

Luke 1:46-55

MY SOUL PROCLAIMS THE GREATNESS OF THE LORD,

MY SPIRIT REJOICES IN GOD MY SAVIOR,

FOR HE HAS LOOKED WITH FAVOR ON HIS LOWLY SERVANT.

FROM THIS DAY ALL GENERATIONS WILL CALL ME BLESSED:

THE ALMIGHTY HAS DONE GREAT THINGS FOR ME,

AND HOLY IS HIS NAME.

HE HAS MERCY ON THOSE WHO FEAR HIM IN EVERY GENERATION.

HE HAS SHOWN THE STRENGTH OF HIS ARM,

HE HAS SCATTERED THE PROUD IN THEIR CONCEIT.

HE HAS CAST DOWN THE MIGHTY FROM THEIR THRONES,

AND HAS LIFTED UP THE LOWLY.

HE HAS FILLED THE HUNGRY WITH GOOD THINGS,

AND THE RICH HE HAS SENT AWAY EMPTY.

HE HAS COME TO THE HELP OF HIS SERVANT ISRAEL,

FOR HE REMEMBERED HIS PROMISE OF MERCY,

THE PROMISE HE MADE TO OUR FATHERS,

TO ABRAHAM AND HIS CHILDREN FOREVER.

LITANY OF HUMILITY

O JESUS! MEEK AND HUMBLE OF HEART, HEAR ME.

FROM THE DESIRE OF BEING ESTEEMED, DELIVER ME, O JESUS.

FROM THE DESIRE OF BEING LOVED, DELIVER ME, O JESUS.

FROM THE DESIRE OF BEING EXTOLLED, DELIVER ME, O JESUS.

FROM THE DESIRE OF BEING HONORED, DELIVER ME, O JESUS.

FROM THE DESIRE OF BEING PRAISED, DELIVER ME, O JESUS.

FROM THE DESIRE OF BEING PREFERRED TO OTHERS, DELIVER ME, O JESUS.

FROM THE DESIRE OF BEING CONSULTED, DELIVER ME, O JESUS.

FROM THE DESIRE OF BEING APPROVED, DELIVER ME, O JESUS.

FROM THE FEAR OF BEING HUMILIATED, DELIVER ME, O JESUS.

FROM THE FEAR OF BEING DESPISED, DELIVER ME, O JESUS.

FROM THE FEAR OF SUFFERING REBUKES, DELIVER ME, O JESUS.

FROM THE FEAR OF BEING CALUMNIATED, DELIVER ME, O JESUS.

FROM THE FEAR OF BEING FORGOTTEN, DELIVER ME, O JESUS.

FROM THE FEAR OF BEING RIDICULED, DELIVER ME, O JESUS.

FROM THE FEAR OF BEING WRONGED, DELIVER ME, O JESUS.

FROM THE FEAR OF BEING SUSPECTED, DELIVER ME, O JESUS.

THAT OTHERS MAY BE LOVED MORE THAN I, JESUS, GRANT ME THE GRACE TO DESIRE IT.

THAT OTHERS MAY BE ESTEEMED MORE THAN I, JESUS, GRANT ME THE GRACE TO DESIRE IT.

THAT, IN THE OPINION OF THE WORLD, OTHERS MAY INCREASE AND I MAY DECREASE,

JESUS, GRANT ME THE GRACE TO DESIRE IT.

THAT OTHERS MAY BE CHOSEN AND I SET ASIDE, JESUS, GRANT ME THE GRACE TO DESIRE IT.

THAT OTHERS MAY BE PRAISED AND I UNNOTICED, JESUS, GRANT ME THE GRACE TO DESIRE IT.

THAT OTHERS MAY BE PREFERRED TO ME IN EVERYTHING, JESUS, GRANT ME THE GRACE TO DESIRE IT.

THAT OTHERS MAY BECOME HOLIER THAN I, PROVIDED THAT I MAY BECOME AS HOLY AS I SHOULD,

JESUS, GRANT ME THE GRACE TO DESIRE IT.

LITANY OF TRUST

Written by the Sisters of Life (SistersOfLife.org)

FROM THE BELIEF THAT I HAVE TO EARN YOUR LOVE, DELIVER ME, JESUS.

FROM THE FEAR THAT I AM UNLOVABLE, DELIVER ME, JESUS.

FROM THE FALSE SECURITY THAT I HAVE WHAT IT TAKES, DELIVER ME, JESUS.

FROM THE FEAR THAT TRUSTING YOU WILL LEAVE ME MORE DESTITUTE, DELIVER ME, JESUS.

FROM ALL SUSPICION OF YOUR WORDS AND PROMISES, DELIVER ME, JESUS.

FROM THE REBELLION AGAINST CHILDLIKE DEPENDENCY ON YOU, DELIVER ME, JESUS.

FROM REFUSALS AND RELUCTANCES IN ACCEPTING YOUR WILL, DELIVER ME, JESUS.

FROM ANXIETY ABOUT THE FUTURE, DELIVER ME, JESUS.

FROM RESENTMENT OR EXCESSIVE PREOCCUPATION WITH THE PAST, DELIVER ME, JESUS.

FROM RESTLESS SELF-SEEKING IN THE PRESENT MOMENT, DELIVER ME, JESUS.

FROM DISBELIEF IN YOUR LOVE AND PRESENCE, DELIVER ME, JESUS.

FROM THE FEAR OF BEING ASKED TO GIVE MORE THAN I HAVE, DELIVER ME, JESUS.

FROM THE BELIEF THAT MY LIFE HAS NO MEANING OR WORTH, DELIVER ME, JESUS.

FROM THE FEAR OF WHAT LOVE DEMANDS, DELIVER ME, JESUS.

FROM DISCOURAGEMENT, DELIVER ME, JESUS.

THAT YOU ARE CONTINUALLY HOLDING ME, SUSTAINING ME, LOVING ME, JESUS, I TRUST IN YOU.

THAT YOUR LOVE GOES DEEPER THAN MY SINS AND FAILINGS AND TRANSFORMS ME, JESUS, I TRUST IN YOU.

THAT NOT KNOWING WHAT TOMORROW BRINGS IS AN INVITATION TO LEAN ON YOU, JESUS, I TRUST IN YOU.

THAT YOU ARE WITH ME IN MY SUFFERING, JESUS, I TRUST IN YOU.

THAT MY SUFFERING, UNITED TO YOUR OWN, WILL BEAR FRUIT IN THIS LIFE AND THE NEXT,
JESUS, I TRUST IN YOU.

THAT YOU WILL NOT LEAVE ME ORPHAN, THAT YOU ARE PRESENT IN YOUR CHURCH, JESUS, I TRUST IN YOU.

THAT YOUR PLAN IS BETTER THAN ANYTHING ELSE, JESUS, I TRUST IN YOU.

THAT YOU ALWAYS HEAR ME AND IN YOUR GOODNESS ALWAYS RESPOND TO ME, JESUS, I TRUST IN YOU.

THAT YOU GIVE ME THE GRACE TO ACCEPT FORGIVENESS AND TO FORGIVE OTHERS, JESUS, I TRUST IN YOU.

THAT YOU GIVE ME ALL THE STRENGTH I NEED FOR WHAT IS ASKED, JESUS, I TRUST IN YOU.

THAT MY LIFE IS A GIFT, JESUS, I TRUST IN YOU.

THAT YOU WILL TEACH ME TO TRUST YOU, JESUS, I TRUST IN YOU.

THAT YOU ARE MY LORD AND MY GOD, JESUS, I TRUST IN YOU.

THAT I AM YOUR BELOVED ONE, JESUS, I TRUST IN YOU.

Made in United States
Troutdale, OR
01/16/2024

16959007R00159